Photographers Credits

Satoshi Asakawa, Kouji Okamoto,
Shinkenchiku-sha, Yoshio Shiratori,
Yoshio Takase, Shoei Yoh

Editorial Director USA
Pierantonio Giacoppo

Chief Editor of Collection
Maurizio Vitta

Publishing Coordinator
Franca Rottola

Graphic Design
Paola Polastri

Editing
Jesse Oona Nickerson
Martyn J. Anderson

Colour-separation
Litofilms Italia, Bergamo

Printing
Poligrafiche Bolis, Bergamo

First published February 1997

ISBN 88-7838-022-9

Shoei Yoh

Shoei Yoh

In Response to Natural Phenomena

Text by
Anthony Iannacci

Introductions by
Kisho Kurokawa
Greg Lynn
Shoei Yoh

Contents

Architecture as Legacy

by Kisho Kurokawa

Tadao Ando and Shoei Yoh are two extraordinary Japanese architects. Ando, who taught himself how to be an architect after a career in boxing, has created a unique architectural world. Shoei Yoh studied economics at Kelo University, and then studied art in the U.S.A. He, too, is a self-taught architect who has created an exceptional architectural world.

Both of these architects share a craftsman's attention to details and materials. To highlight one difference, however, Ando emphasizes concrete materials through the use of simplified details, creating drama in the spaces that are created, through the light and shadow that emerge from the use of these restrictions. Yoh, on the other hand, deliberately rises to the challenge of working with all types of materials, including metal, wood, glass, and concrete. He continues to work with an extremely wide range of structural types as well, including shell and hanging structures, wooden trusses, and bonded construction techniques.

The world is currently in the midst of a major paradigm shift, the likes of which take place no more than once every several hundred years. In addition to the end of the U.S. /Soviet Cold War and the crumbling of the Berlin wall, an avalanche of change is taking place in all fields, including politics, economics, science, technology, art, and culture. In scholarly fields as well, walls are crumbling between the areas of

specialization that existed in the past, as all fields of expertise are beginning to intermingle. The free-spirited Shoei Yoh, who has worked without concerning himself with boundaries between economics, art, and architecture, is indeed a fitting creator of this new age.

Where is the paradigm shift of this age leading? I consider the 21st-century world order to be an age of symbiosis, and the architecture of this new age to be one of symbiosis, or intercultural architecture.

The modern age moved toward the goal of an industrialized society: I refer to this age as the age of the machine. As machines were mass produced we moved closer to our goal of global culture, and thus the individuality of architects, their natural and cultural diversity, became relatively insignificant.

The age of symbiosis is an age that is capable of bridging dualistic oppositions such as globalism and regionalism, universality and individuality, or nature and technology. Scholarly systems on which modern architecture has been founded, including the bourbakian systems of Kant, Newton, Darwin, Lavoisier, and Euclid, are giving way to new, non-bourbakian scholarly systems of symbiosis and non-dualism. Fractal geometry demonstrated that the order of a whole is revealed in its parts in the manner of nested inserts. It has already been demonstrated that there is no essential difference between the randomness that is found in nature and the regularity found in geometry and mathematics.

The secret order hidden within complex systems are being revealed by Koestler's holon, Haken's synergetics, and the soliton wave as a phenomenon of resonance.

I also call this new age the age of life principles. I have based my architectural work on the key concepts of metabolism, metamorphosis, and symbiosis, because these are the most fundamental principles of life.

Looking at these principles on the basis of their forms, it is clear that they are complex and diverse.

Neither the negative influence of postmodernism nor fin-de-siècle confusion is responsible for the fact that the world's architecture is becoming more diverse rather than converging on any one style. I believe this is nothing more than a demonstration that architecture is moving toward the age of life principles and the order that is found in complex systems. Like the other architects who have looked toward this type of new age - Eisenman, Tschumi, Shirdel, and Calatrava - Shoei Yoh seems also to be instinctively anticipating a new age of symbiosis and life principles.

Just as life can be defined as "a site which generates meaning while maintaining relationships with its continually changing surroundings," the architecture of life principles creates complex, free forms by reflecting the "noise", the cultural context of the site. For example, in the roof of the

Odawara sports complex, or the roof of the glass station at Oguni-machi, designed by Shoei Yoh, effects of nature such as snow accumulation, heat, and wind are considered indifferentially determining each part of the roof's structure.

Yoh has said that his own works are "architecture for the enjoyment of nature, a Japanese tradition." Japanese culture, of course, includes formal and artistic traditions that are visible to the eye, but it places even more emphasis on ones that are intangible. These include aesthetic consciousness, life style, and philosophy.

I believe the reason for the tendency of Japanese architects to actively incorporate the latest materials, structures, and technologies in their work actually reveals a need to maintain an intangible, traditional, aesthetic consciousness and philosophy. Shoei Yoh's concept of "architecture for the enjoyment of nature" can be viewed as a continuation of the spirit of Japanese gardens and sukiya-zukuri tea houses, which are created with a sensitivity to natural light, wind, and sound.

In Shirdel's competition proposal for the Convention Hall in Nara, an original analysis of the structure of Todaiji Temple was converted into a new spatial composition using a computer. This resulted in the creation of a new architectural work using external, cultural, rather than natural data, since it involves digitalizing a

traditional Japanese ideal and manipulating it for expression in a modern work of architecture.

Greg Lynn has stated in an essay (Architectural Design Profile No. 102) that the work of Shoei Yoh has something in common with that of mine. Creating symbiosis among heterogeneous elements, external elements of a different dimension and architecture, can also be described as the creation of relationships. The deconstruction of architecture is not in itself enough to create new spaces. The question is what sorts of relationships those elements are given after deconstruction, and whether a new order is achieved through some medium. I have paid attention in my work to the interval or "ma" between entities, the intermediate domain, because I am interested in the relationships between entities rather than in the entities themselves. In the architecture of Shoei Yoh, an element of natural randomness is incorporated into a computerized matrix to lend irregularity to an HP shell structure or a lattice structure. In other words, this could be viewed as an experiment using existing geometrical systems or structural styles to create a more complex, freer form.

Up until the present, Shoei Yoh has designed relatively small-scale buildings which are rather simple in function. His activities, however will no doubt become international in scope as he takes up the challenge of larger-scale works in the future.

To what extent will the methods he has developed so far be applicable at that time? Of course, Yoh is aware that architecture cannot exist in harmony only with nature, the outside.

He is now working on the area in which he is most skilled. In transposing the natural parameters of light, wind, and air into the infinitely complex parameters of society, there will be a need for an element other than the medium of the structure. This element will most likely be his own thinking with respect to the culture of the place where the building is located. The architecture that is most likely to remain as a legacy for the next generation is work that embodies the spirit of the age.

Only architecture that testifies to its era merits preservation as a cultural asset. Paris's Eiffel Tower, the world's first skyscraper observation tower, speaks of its era through its very structure and material, cast iron.

In many cases, the works of architecture that embody the spirit of their age reflect the philosophy, art, and culture of that time, for example, Notre Dame cathedral, and many of Florence's Renaissance buildings.

If there is any new architecture, it cannot be a materialistic, noumenal architecture with a form that has never existed in the past.

Both Tadao Ando and Shoei Yoh face challenging hurdles, but, they face them with anticipation. I look forward to watching them rise to meet those challenges.

Classicism and Vitality

by Greg Lynn

Throughout his career, Shoei Yoh has attempted to capture and reproduce natural effects and forces through architectural constructions.

There are two possible trajectories for an architecture that models itself on nature. The first is a classical tradition that essentializes nature through methods of reduction to primitive object types. The second tradition is not classical but combinative; it looks to processes of formalization that combine multiple interacting systems, from which complex methodologies are set into motion, which behave like an ecology of components exhibiting collective behavior and regulation. Whereas the classical tradition is dependent on the existence of natural forms, the combinative tradition depends on modes of formalization.

Shoei Yoh's work exhibits tendencies toward the classical embodiment of organic forms as well as toward a more vital construction of form through multiple elements. Although one does not find a linear trajectory from the classical to the combinative, there has been a progressive development from reductive Cartesianism toward the more complex and topological methods of design he uses presently. His early work, from the mid to late 1970's, reveals an intense frustration with the dogma of modernism, even more so, of Corbusian Purism, demands that his early work be read as a reaction to the classical tenants of high modern architecture.

It will be argued later that his work developed along a more experimental trajectory, one that breaks away from both the groundedness or orientation and the formal idealism of the classical tradition of refinement and reduction. Like the work of many of his peers during the 1970's, his early work, however, must be understood as a critical reaction within the logic of late modernism. Later in this text it will be argued that Yoh has recently exceeded these classical limits of ground plane and Cartesian volume by developing a vocabulary of topological roof forms and landscaped beams.

But before launching these arguments about his work it is necessary to start by identifying his reaction to the classical impulses of late modernism.

Before discussing this reaction, it is necessary to understand the broad architectural context for this work. Yoh was not only responding to the dominant late modern architecture that preceded him, but also to more recent developments that extended the modern tradition along new lines. Strategies involving the collision, superimposition, and erosion of spheres, cubes, pyramids, etc., had been exhaustively described by Colin Rowe and Robert Slutzky in the mid 1960's, and these strategies had been developed by the New York Five, among others. At the same time the Metabolists, the first avant-garde movement in Japanese architecture, were combining many of the Team 10 urban strategies with new formal morphologies. In both cases there was simultaneously a continuity with a predominantly Corbusian tradition and a kind of hyperdevelopment of, in the case of Rowe, formalism, and, in the case of the Metabolists, urban superstructures. While certain aesthetic affinities can be found between Yoh's work and that of the Metabolists and the Five, it is most interesting to argue in very broad terms that there was both an impulse to continue the modern project and some kind of mutation or hyperdevelopment of modernism along alternative lines. What can be shown quite conclusively is that despite the innovations in many regards, there was a definitive maintenance of the most classical and conservative aspects of modern architecture, a datum of ideal forms on a horizontal ground.

Yoh's initial research into alternative pure object types was linked to research into substitute strategies for support and movement within those forms. The manner in which the primary forms of cylinders, cubes, pyramids and spheres are rotated, sliced, and suspended under, in, and above the ground indicated a criticism of horizontal grounding. His work not only developed a new language of pure forms, but it also developed new techniques for arranging those volumes unconventionally in space.

This combination of new object types and an innovative placement of those pure forms on the ground points to the complex dependency between essential Platonic solids and a horizontal tableau upon which they are composed.

This relationship between primitive forms and their support and placement was criticized by Yoh's early work. This criticism anticipated his later departure from Cartesian geometries, as well as his adoption of topological surfaces instead of closed volumes.

It must be said that Yoh's work with topological surfaces is among the first in Japan or elsewhere, and these surfaces are the consequence of many of the limits discovered in his early work. This work takes on an "eccentric" reading of Corbusianism. The term "eccentric" is not meant to suggest a deviant form of expressionism outside the boundaries of good form, but more literally and structurally, an orientation that is more of less off-center. In numerous projects, eccentricities can be found both in the use of Cartesian volumes that are not centered and in the relationship of these volumes to the ground in a sloped or diagonal manner.

The Kinoshita Clinic of 1979, for example, is not a sphere but an oblong ovoid which is only tentatively supported on the surface of the earth like an inverted meniscus. Here the volume of the project is an attenuated sphere without a single center, as ovoids

have at least four centers, and the grounding of this volume is on a tangent to its surface. It is not embedded in the ground, as its envelope does not engage any foundations — instead it slips across the surface like an egg in a manner that is coincident or coplanar with the earth's surface. Similarly, the Ingot Coffee Shop is a single cubical volume rotated 40 degrees so that it rests on its edge.

Unlike the glass houses of Mies van der Rohe and Philip Johnson (not to mention the work of a recent spate of mannered imitators, such as Nouvel and Herzog), Yoh chose to situate the space obliquely rather than on a positive or negative plinth, as did Johnson and Mies respectively.

Other projects, ones which do not rethink the problem of support and ground, focus instead on a research into volumes that are monolithic without being reducible or Platonic. This points to the tendency in Yoh's work to idealize nature through both organic forms and physical processes. His quasi-naturalistic forms have an affinity with the structures of Wright and Goff in that they attempt to articulate essential formal types through natural or organic metaphors rather than through mathematical or geometrical statements. These naturalistic object types are geometrically derived nonetheless, through Cartesian volumetric means.

The limitation of these more organic forms is that they are

as essentialized as the object types they replace, and that they mimic natural forms. These examples are more limited in Yoh's work and include the long-span project for the Oguni Dome, which Yoh has described as a crustacean; the Misumi Kumamoro Ferry Terminal, which uses a three-dimensional spiral for its organization; and finally the ziggurat form of the Egami Clinic.

Yoh has consistently involved the expression on natural forces and forms in his work. The rejection of Platonic forms in his early work, in favor of organization more tied to organicism, is just one example.

Yet this work, as it became more organic, became more conventionally oriented and sited. Whereas in the early projects one found an oppositional strategy of placing volumes in an oblique or eccentric relationship to the ground, the more organic object types lost that critical grounding and sat in a horizontal relationship to the ground.

The critical edge in this regard was recovered at the same time that the projects developed a more subtle relationship with land forms themselves. The major break in Yoh's work, a break away from the classical tradition, coincided with his use of flexible topological surfaces. In the topological projects, the buildings themselves take on landscapelike characteristics in both their forms and their formation. This is the important relationship between formalization and

formation, where the roof profiles were generated out of the interaction of multiple independent requirements and thus manifest undulating, organic contours. In this way the projects appear natural in that each forms a heterogeneous yet continuous surface that never duplicates a single contour, while retaining a degree of repetition. This does not make the projects natural, yet their forms invite naturalistic readings at the aesthetic level. The ability of these projects to appear natural, or to mimic nature, no doubt played a major role in their use by Yoh. The degree to which they became like landscape forms would raise Yoh's earlier question as to the building's relationship to the ground. In two other texts I have discussed these projects in greater detail [1-2], but their general implications can be summarized through a description of any one of the projects. To take the Odawara Sports Complex as an example, it develops an intricate and differential relationship to both program and structure in order to generate a roof form which has a relationship to the surrounding mountainous landscape that is more of a land form than a discrete object. In the Odawara Sports Complex, the Galaxy Toyama Gymnasium, the Glass Station, the Naiju Community Center and Nursery School, and the Uchino Community Center, the roof form of the projects can be characterized as having a highly differentiated globular singularity. In all of these

projects there is a response to the shifts in the economies and techniques of construction from one of assembly-line production of a standard to the assembly-like production of a series of singular units. These projects articulate an approach to standardization and repetition that combines a generic system of construction with slight variations of each member. This attribute is reminiscent of historic methods of craftsmanship where every element could be generic in some regard while given a distinct identity at each instance.

In some of the projects, inexpensive craftsmanship and indigenous techniques were employed in favor of mechanical fabrication techniques. Methods of bamboo form-work construction is one such example. Most of these projects make use of both prefabricated steel components and site-fabricated bamboo and concrete. Through both manual construction and industrial fabrication they exploit the economies of what is often referred to as "custom assembly-line production." A spatial theme evident in all of Yoh's recent work is the enclosure of a diverse group of programs under a single roof. The conventional approach to this problem would be to identify either a maximum or an average span for a roof height that could then be used for the entire structure. Rather than simplifying the roof structure to an ideal module that would be repeated identically, Yoh respected the specificity of each program and developed a surface that would continuously connect across all of these heights like a wet cloth. The structural members of this system are similar but not identical. This strategy uses both a generic and particular approach. There is repetition, but with each repetition of a homogeneous surface there is a slight fluctuation or differentiation.

This multiplicity of minor variations does not add up to a single, simple global structure, but instead manifests a singularity that constantly fluctuates across its surface locally. These projects of Shoei Yoh subtly complicate the distinctions between a global system and local components, between the general structure and particular variations, and even between industrialized fabrication techniques and indigenous construction. The variations in the global form are the result of local variations in the program, and these variations are taken up in a repetitive construction technique where every element is slightly differentiated within a more or less continuous system. They are both continuous and heterogeneous in their shape and construction. This combination of microheterogeneity and differentiation with macrocontinuity and inflection leads to their appearance as landscapes or natural formations.

These projects mark a new direction for Yoh and others, in their use of topological surfaces rather than Cartesian volumes.

These surfaces raise a series of complex relationships between interior and exterior, between ground and figure, between surface and volume, and between repetition and differentiation. Until this moment, the research into these forms of organization has been limited to long-span roof structures. In order to analyze the relationships of these roof forms to the ground, one is limited to the transition from ceiling to wall to landscape, and in the end these readings are inevitably unsatisfying.

The diagonal walls of the Galaxy Toyama Gymnasium and the Saarinen-like piers of the Glass Station seem to barely scratch the surface of the potential for new relationships between these topologies and the earth.

In order to truly exploit the possibilities   of these new forms of organization and support Yoh must not limit the strategies to roofs only. In the same way the Cartesian volumes were reoriented and used to structure space in an unconventional manner, so too might these topologies suggest new strategies for spatial enclosure.

From the early criticism of late modern object types and their relationship to the ground, Yoh has moved into the uncharted territory of topological surfaces. From the metaphors of natural forms and forces he developed a method of complex formation that is organic in its combination of multiple interaction constraints. In both regards, his recent work is presently

unprecedented and has managed to escape the envelope of the merely modern. This is a heroic feat at this time, as, almost a century after its inception, the modern movement still has currency as a mode of inquiry. Many architects claim to be doing experimental work by refining the aesthetic language of Mies or Corbusier. Yoh grappled with those precedents in the early 1970's and, after having exhausted those strategies, he moved into new territories of structure, construction, function, and form based on topology and flexible surfaces. He is one of the few architects who have chosen and defined a new set of issues to experiment with, issues that are more relevant and vital than those of the now-tired modern movement.

[1]"Architectural Curvilinearity: the Folded, the Pliant and the Supple" in Folding in Architecture: Architectural Design Profile no. 102 (London: Academy Group Ltd., 1993) pp. 8-16

[2]"Blob Tectonics of Why Tectonics is Square and Topology is Groovy" in Tectonics Unbound: Any Magazine. (New York: Any Corp.. 1996).

Architecture in Motion

by Shoei Yoh

In the decade of the 60's, the walking city of Archigram, the aircraft career of Hans Hollein, and the continuous monuments of Super Studio were unconventional, shocking presentations that affected the architectural scenes. Recently, I have been recalling those days, thirty years later, as I've found no constant and stable architectural persistence as time passes.

They predicted right.

Oriental thoughts express similar concepts. Though the former may be dynamic and the latter static.

In any case, to start with, there had always been a premise of "constant stability" in our mind, however, I hardly see the beginning nor the end, but just a "process" of existence.

Sometimes an evolution may be seen like a living creature, but only an aging one in most cases.

In a process of birth and death, there is living for a while. So it is in architecture. In order to survive long, I believe that it would be better to be supple physically and metaphysically. "Arcitecture in Motion" now finds itself phenomenologically levitating, breathing, stretching, distorting, swaying and meandering just as is proved by my twenty-five years of work . "Architecture in Motion" is always a process of charging and discharging the energy to live on.

Restoration, alteration, adaptation and programming-unprogramming may revitalize architecture.

All of these motions could be carried out through my "callisthenics for architecture" as I introduce it here[1].

Practice and exercise to keep in shape is supposedly required, since it is easy to deform and collapse, as a square easily distorts unless its joints are stiffened. We tend to misunderstand a square in a stable condition sitting on ground.

A triangle never deforms, but on the contrary, a square is always in motion, keeping energy over time. Stiffening the square to obtain rigidity from swaying and changing angles at the corners all the time takes a lot of effort.

Just like in traditional Japanese architecture, the heavy weight of the roof sometimes helps. It's an analogy of the Oriental society in a chaotic highly dense city, keeping the individual members free by changing relationships.

A soft and supple mutual relationship between the others would well-preserve architecture's individual originality in a society whose rigidity or stiffness may not respond well to functional and social changes.

An interface such as a fish scale enclosing soft bodies, or silicone joints for hard glass panes on hard steel structures, show what I've been intending.

No matter how solid, hard or rigid an architecture is, it has to be in motion to survive.

Both internal and external forces are constantly and inevitably deforming and distorting architecture, until it collapses.

Its life depends on its fluidity, its ability to catch up and to respond to phenomenological changes.

Surviving in an Explosive-Chaotic City

An explosion of population will be seen in the Asian cities at the end of this century and the beginning of the next.

Living and working in high density cities seems almost to be chaos, however it is not avoidable, there is no choice involved.

Here I would urgently like to make a survival proposal of how to live and work in a dense city without compromising, enjoying the high culture and efficient convenience that only a city can afford us, as well as the affluent solar light for babies and the elderly. It is an alternative utopia of co-existing in highly mixed-use cities with plenty of open spaces, like Central Park in NY.

I've reached the idea through a careful study of building shadows, especially the multiple ones in a redeveloping area in Minato Ward in Tokyo.

In the Northern hemisphere, I propose to save the south side of high-rise buildings for living and the north for working.

A living unit is hardly ever deeper than 12 m due to natural daylight and air, but on the other hand, an office can be 20-30 m deep with an ideal constant climate of air- conditioning and artificial lighting. An office is normally used only eight hours a day, five days a week and is vacant for the rest of the day and the weekend.

There would be no disadvantage to living in the south 365 days, and to working in the north eight hours a day for 200 days. It is a form of sharing.

To get together from all over the countryside to the cities means sharing time, space, sunshine, daylight, energy and even communication with others.

It is now realized in my high-rise. Strict separation of time and space in cities has been an agenda for city planning prevailing all over no more effective.

In this millennium, a pair of Chop-sticks (HASHI) and a rotating round table may take over sets of knives, forks and spoons.

Equality is found in high efficiency. Living together in a dense city, we are to share diversity of ethnics, religion, and values. It has been a surprise to me to find no other preceding examples based on this idea, to the best of my knowledge. (PAT)

Since an elevator as vertical transportation was introduced at the beginning of the 20th century, all the cities started to raise buildings higher and higher, allowing for higher density in a limited space, in cities like NY, sacrificing natural climatic benefits especially the "Sun" for the elderly and babies who live in a city.

Provided the high-rise is inevitable for cities with more than 500% density, we are supposed to raise a building so that we can obtain more open space around it, as well as "sun", "air" and "greenery" for us to walk and enjoy flowers in.

Thus the ground level is liberated for pedestrians.

Our high-rise is for us to enjoy a vast open space around it. Open space was dedicated to traditional city life, in the 19th century, without traffic signs, and before the elevator or the automobile occupied cities. Underground is service space. Old market life?

Fine. Full of flowers? Of course. Siesta under a tree? Why not?

Only one condition for it is to live in the south and work in the north in a high-rise or two high-rises back to back, away from all the others.

If we are able to raise vehicle traffic in the air as high as the middle of high-rise buildings, as I proposed for the city of Yokohama in 1992, it would be perfect.

The conjunction of vertical and horizontal traffic will become a "node" with a marketplace or an atrium-lobby at the intermediate height of a high-rise tower.

It will reduce the number of elevators and will generate a communicating transit-plaza. A city in the air.

It would be more attractive if we could have an open space as tall as 3-4 stories to give a bird's-eye view to see the active marketplace where we go around with escalators to go up and down for shopping or eating. This aereal city has not been realized yet either. (PAT)

Surviving in a chaotic, high-density city would certainly have to introduce such an aerial city of high-rises with a vast, free, open space around it.

Is this too optimistic?

Levitating and Anchored Architecture

In 1977, I designed a coffee shop (4x4x22m) called Ingot, a monolith of black, shiny metallic glass, placed at fourty degrees on a slope in the woods.

Seventeen years later, I designed four wooden prisms (6x6x24) sticking out 12 m from a hill.

All of a sudden I found the buildings I designed with geometric forms looked somehow as though they were levitating.

The relationship between the site and the building is supposed to generate a magnetic field. If there is a black hole everything will be absorbed as + or -, in these cases of + and +, or - and -, my geometric self-completed architecture form appears to me to be levitating in the air, an astonishing visual effect.

Instability and uncertain lightness in buildings is in contrast with the heavy weight of the site and the historical and cultural context. That's the intention, like the portable tent of a nomad is only a temporary presence.

Following Oriental thinking concerning our temporary dwelling in the universe, I have been trying to respect the significance of the site. As a part of nature, blowing in the wind, and scorched by the sun, we are constantly rebelling against gravity in some way or another such as with cantilevers, suspensions, or pilotis.

That's why some of my buildings don't seem heavy enough to remain on certain sites, because they are empty inside their geometric form of enclosure. Teleportion may be considered as they don't belong to any specific site.

Those geometric forms also cause us to lose our sense of scale, no matter how huge or tiny, they can exist even without a sense of scale. In other words, purity of form tends to be looked at as an object rather than a building belonging to a specific site.

Neutrality is now emphasized in the relationship between natural landscaping and the object. "Space and Time" are intended as a neutral effect.

Some day, levitating architecture might fly away, therefore sometimes we might need an intentional anchor.

In the "Glass Station", made of concrete and a 3D glass membrane, which is run and owned by people who live in the concrete cube office located in front, both are firmly anchored at the "gate" of a forest town, in a valley with a river running in its center.

The forest town of Oguni is well-known in this country for its very big wooden gymnasium, which I designed ten years ago.

In this town it is a must for an architect to use wood.

However, I designed both buildings in concrete which cannot be substituted with any other material, as they live off the concrete business.

There is a mutual relationship of + and - between building and site. Both are very tightly connected. The buildings, composing a gate, are now anchored in this way.

Phenomenological Architecture

Through my works, starting from 1990, in the Toyama Prefecture building, my liberation from the ancient geometric approach to architecture has been examined .

When a heavy snow load started to bend the roof and deformed it as the computer had simulated, we used a heavier steel section to stiffen the structure and never thought of modifying the depth of the truss.

In the case of the Toyama Galaxy 92, I was suddenly inspired to vary the depth of the truss in response to the bending until it became stiff enough, as shown in our computer-simulated drawing.

Surprisingly, this automatic deformation made by the snow load shows us an unusual irregular form, which the snow load decided automatically. Deformation of a conventional flat truss roof structure tells us what to do next, in concern to the waterflow pitch on the roof.

Therefore I relocated some supporting columns, and changed the proportion above and below the center line. It's a fluid and open system structure, a far cry from rigid geometries.

In response to natural phenomena, we are able to deform geometry to reach optimum form, which is also economical and efficient in an age of highly industrial technology.

The optimum form is rational, and economical. It minimizes the volume of steel to be consumed for sustainable community design, that reduces CO_2.

It is just the beginning of Phenomenological Architecture: a given form can look like a cloud in the sky or a galaxy in the universe.

In our next project, the Odawara Sports Complex, we employed external forces such as snow and wind load, as well as a few more disparate acoustic, lighting and program requirements.

The discontinuity between part and whole, external forces and internal requirements gives us a most complex and compliant character in the smooth fluidity system. As Gregg Lynn points out, "this aqueous paradigm seems to indicate the development of a more supple, pliant, open, involved and intense alternative to the familiar practices of formal conflict, violence and contradiction in architecture".

Our third trial was the "Glass Station" with a three-dimensional minimum surface membrane glass canopy for a gas station. (PAT)

It's a glass bubble with a pre-stressed steel wire net which resists the snow and wind load. Four concrete arches were automatically derived along the street, and the glass bubble inside the four arches was also computer-programmed and simulated, after examination in a wind tunnel.

The movement against wind and snow loads is extremely limited when compared with a two-dimensional, flat, glass screen with stressed steel wire of the same kind, like the atrium of the airport hotel in Munich by Helmut Jahn, which moves more than 1 m against the wind.

Our fourth trial was a square bamboo net, hung on a temporary central post. Gravity decides the form with a lot of folds after being stretched and anchored to the ground foundation. The square of the bamboo grid thoroughly kept even when the whole shape deformed.

At first it was a tensile bamboo structure bearing a wet concrete load. Three weeks later it became a compressive concrete shell dome stiffened by foldings after the removal of the central post.

This free form of a giant bamboo handkerchief in a square with foldings is another example of natural phenomena responding to architecture.

In a way it seems very primitive as it is far away from the geometric approach which is supposed to be scientific and civilized.

However, this was made possible only by computer analysis. Foldings are more than effective structurally, useful as openings, and also as alcoves and niches which have comfortable features for children and the elderly. In these alcoves an acoustic effect similar to those experienced by a human ear is attained.

The bamboo net, after its usage, is left in memory of those who helped make it a member of the community of Naiju: i.e., all the graduates of the primary school that was originally located on this site for almost a hundred years.

The fifth trial was the Uchino Community Center, also for kids and the elderly, who are welcomed by a soft embracing space made of bamboo net whose grid is not at a right angle anymore due to the curved concrete vault and dome shell deforming all the squares for a three-dimensional form without foldings, unlike the one in Naiju.

It's a shell with a brim around it to give the roof stiffness, just like the tie-bars of old vault buildings, and also to give a roofed space around the building as an arcade.

The plan is no longer on a grid but just free with a continuous supporting line of columns keeping glass sliding door openings in between the columns all the way around for people to go in and out any time, anywhere.

The form of the roof was given automatically by the plan, the wider the room inside, the higher the roof and ceiling. The soft edge, like the brim of a hat, sways up to stop the rain and down for drainage. This free open plan under a shell is similar to Frei Otto's wooden lattice shell in Mannheim, however the fluttering edge stiffener cantilevered outside of the supporting line is our own unique idea, as far as I know. (PAT)

All of these parameters are based on natural phenomena to reorganize these architecture forms following a hierarchy created by me. It is based on an intentional order of my own judgement through interactive simulation.

The optimum form or solution doesn't always provide an alternative choice, however arbitrariness, to me seems still unlimited, even if the optimum solution excludes it. Here are the possible unlimited varieties of my thoughts which Jeffrey Kipnis would not have been optimistic enough to admit[2].

This kind of Phenomenological Architecture could be much more flexible, like the roll of rectangular free-size KIMONO textile covers that clothes any shape body, as well as the square textile FUROSHIKI, that wraps anything. Any shape provided for the foldings over wrapping plaits or gathering is with no doubt rational. On the other hand the square or rectangular shape can easily be deformed by changing its angles from 90° to any other different degrees.

Instead the rigid triangle never deforms, it can be compared, more or less along western principles, to a hard and clear crystal, instead of the flexible, uncertain, ambiguous and amorphous eastern thoughts, which resemble liquid.

Chaotic dynamism in the East which is again Phenomenatic, rather than static geometry, generates internal forces with the passing of time. The essence of JUDOH is how to utilize the overwhelming power of the competitior, or the external force, as a counterpower to beat or to react to in turn. Internal and external forces correspond.

These Oriental thoughts may be reflected and found in my Phenomenological Architecture responding to natural phenomena, which is a deforming and always temporary process, constantly changing and never static as time introduces tremendous diversities.

In the process, nothing is permanent or eternal in our Oriental thoughts. Dynamic deformation of architecture is inevitable sooner or later, due to physical and social changes. One of my intentions is to absorb the shock of changes or the stress that deforms architecture which may be called "Soft Environment", or, "Architecture in Motion".

No architecture can be the same as it was yesterday.

It belongs to an aging process, but however, hopefully, it can be restored and exceptionally preserved, as a part of natural phenomena.

[1]SD Magazine, JAN 1997. "Callisthenics for Architecture" by Shoei Yoh

[2]Architectural design No. 63 "Folding in Architecture"

Works

Ingot Coffee Shop

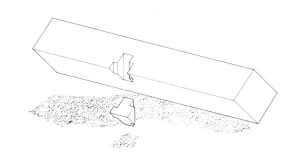

Shoei Yoh's Ingot Coffee shop was completed in Kitakyushu in October of 1977 and dismantled in June of 1986. During its short life the simultaneously reflective and transparent, ingotlike, 4-by-4-by-22 meter construction became not only a symbol of contradictions and developments within contemporary culture, but also an introduction to Yoh's architectural representations of such contradictions. Yoh's parallelepiped structure seemed to sit precariously within the landscape on one of its partially embedded corners. Here no vertical posts, horizontal beams or interior walls were used. There were no gaskets or window sashes to obstruct the view from within: the chromed, heat-absorbing, double-layered glass panels were simply joined to the steel frame with silicone, a technique Yoh introduced into Japan with this project.

Because the panels were not set mechanically into the steel frame, the exterior surface appeared as a continuous, shell-like covering as opposed to an interrupted, structural facade. This project can be seen as the conceptual birthplace of much of Yoh's work that was to follow. Here he introduced a dialogue between structure and form on one hand and between light and natural phenomena on the other, a dialogue that was to become the primary concern of his architecture.

The gleaming, transparent, polished body of the Ingot Coffee Shop introduced Yoh's desire to deny the static rigidity of standard geometry and to embrace a notion of the organic through this negation. Yoh's structure could not be perceived as merely a static, solid geometric form. In the daylight the surface of his Ingot was camouflaged within its setting, the surface became simultaneously dark and bright as it reflected the sky and clouds above and the trees and landscaping of its site.

As the natural sun-light diminished, the interior lights gradually transformed the construction into a glowing framework covered with a thin, transparent glass membrane. Yoh's rigorously geometric parallelepiped maintained the ability to completely lose its form in the darkness, only to recover it again covered with dew in the morning, as if it had undergone some sort of organic metamorphosis.

This building attempted to reduce architecture to a single element, which was then rendered as invisible as possible. For the interior Yoh incorporated transparent tables and chairs and a mirror-faced counter at the entrance, all in an effort to reduce the presence or geometry of the structure. With this onstruction Yoh clearly participated in an architectural representation of contradictions through violent formal and contextual conflicts.

Yoh's building rested lightly on the ground; it seemed merely to appear one day, without any pretense of permanence.

The surrounding
landscape and sky are
here reflected by the
surface of the structure.

The choice of interior
furnishings reflect
the transparency
of the building.

Kinoshita Clinic

Like Yoh's Ingot Coffee Shop, his Kinoshita Clinic, completed in the winter of 1979 in Nishi-ku, Fukuoka Prefecture, set out to question not only certain attitudes about the way in which materials create forms and how those forms are interpreted to create context, but also to question architecture's ability to integrate unrelated elements. Again, like the Ingot Coffee Shop, the Kinoshita Clinic expands into the landscape in a way that is quite uninhibited when compared to traditional architecture. Both structures seem to have neither roof nor foundation; they seem neither stationary nor mobile, and notwithstanding their absolute material and structural distance from nature, they seem to establish a continuum with their site, a continuity grounded in affinities rather than conflicts. Neither of the two constructions was intended as a permanent structure, but it is not for this reason that they maintain this state of integration with their site. Neither has a proper relationship to its surroundings. They mirror the site in neither choice of materials nor form; instead, what integrates them to their sites, is the fact that Yoh has considered both site and construction as disparate, unrelated elements, and has exerted upon them jointly the force of his design.

This 3.6 x 30 x 11-meter oblong, ovoid construction was designed to exist and function until the year 2005. Like some sort of high-tech slug, Yoh's pill-shaped clinic appears to have slowly crawled onto its site from along the coast of Hakata Bay and remained there. Approaching the structure from the northeast, one is drawn to the entrance by a built-up earth ramp that, from this point of view, obscures that fact that much of the structure, with the exception of the portion that seems to lean on the ramp, is suspended some 1.8 meters above the ground. Long before raised floors were used to accommodate changing electrical and technological needs, Yoh suspended this structure to allow for the constant interchange of mechanical equipment and free and easy access for maintenance.

In realizing this project Yoh was challenged by a need to create a functional space despite the restrictions of an oval plan. The limited space in the ovoid construction hosts a central corridor leading to examination rooms and offices that line the parallel sides of the building. At the far, rounded ends of this form Yoh placed the public spaces: an entrance and waiting area at one end, and a semi-open terrace at the other.

Yoh punctured the sculpturally dramatic exterior of the Kinoshita Clinic at intervals along a structural grid. Like a globe, the clinic appears to be covered with latitudinal and longitudinal lines, and sections of this grid have been "cut away" from the solid, ovoid body to reveal an entrance, a terrace, and various curved window surfaces. The exterior needed to be carefully protected from the strong sea winds, and, in part, Yoh's aerodynamic shape reflects this concern. A special polyester surfacing reinforced with glass-fibers and aluminum hydroxide was developed for the continuous exterior facade/roof and cast-in-place silicone hinges were incorporated for the curved glass windows.

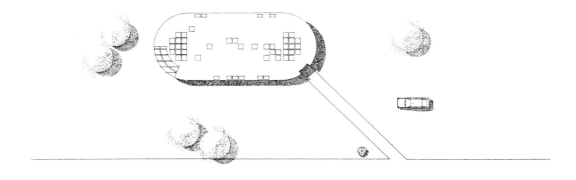

Top, this plan illustrates
the relationship
the building maintains
to the road. Bottom,
the ovoid construction
appears on the site as
if it had crawled there
itself.

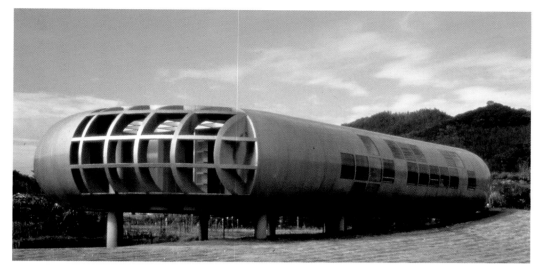

Here the back of the clinic is shown as it rises above the grade to allow for easy access to and maintenance of the building systems below.

Stainless-Steel House with Light Lattice

With his Stainless-Steel House with Light Lattice Yoh introduced his interest in buildings as "environmental systems." His 1980 design for this residence in Higashi-machi, Nagasaki-shi, attempts to extend his dialogue between nature and structure in a new direction.

Yoh observed that progressive industrial technology was making advances by imitating nature, and he attempted to introduce this way of thinking into his architectural practice. For his Stainless-Steel House with Light Lattice, Yoh wanted to create a building with the systems necessary to control its own conditions and attempt to function like living organisms.

Like his Ingot Coffee Shop, the Stainless-Steel House with Light Lattice is again composed of a gridlike steel structure, but here the glass has been reduced to thin strips that lie between the weave of the steel frame. Yoh designed this latticelike structure to be perceived as if it were constructed of light.

Here the double sheets of glass used for the coffee shop have been replaced with rectangular stainless-steel insulation panels, and the solid steel frames have been replaced by two parallel steel frames hosting a narrow strip of transparent glass. Yoh created this complex steel and glass "lattice" from a highly durable 125-millimeter steel channel that was capable of supporting both the lightweight, high performance, factory-made stainless-steel panels constituting the solid facade of the building and the narrow glass strips used to create the "light lattice."

This simultaneously open and closed structure defines the form of the house by functioning not only as structural facade, but also as window, roof, and interior walls and ceiling. For both the Ingot Coffee Shop and the Stainless-Steel House with Light Lattice, Yoh simply fixed the glass or stainless steel to the steel frame with silicone, which both insulates and absorbs movement caused by thermal changes.

Both Ingot Coffee Shop and the Stainless-Steel House with Light Lattice seem to undergo a metamorphosis as the changing effects of light alter their appearance. By day Yoh's coffee shop was a solid of reflecting glass that addressed its site by creating a sort of street theater in the mirror-image it produced of its surroundings. As the natural light diminished, it focused on the building's interior to become transparent and a glowing theater.

Like the facade of Yoh's coffee shop, the glass-filled slots within the stainless-steel clad house also become transparent in the evening as the interior is illuminated, but the effect is radically different here.

Though the difference between them is in part one of mass and volume, the changing relationship to light creates psychological as well as visual effects. Once within the house the effect can be compared to looking at the sunlight as it filters through a shade tree, whereas the experience within the coffee shop can be compared to gazing at light itself. Yoh uses light in his Stainless-Steel House with Light Lattice to indicate the passage of time and to create an architecture that becomes acutely sensitive to environmental changes. During the day the rectangular slits within the lattice create stripes of light within the house, while after sunset the lattice begins to emerge in the night so that the house begins to resemble packaging around a mass of light.

Yoh divided the 125-square-meter house into three zones: a private area on the east; a public area on the west; and a central, glass-enclosed light court. A tatami-floored area within the living room can be made private or can remain as an extension of that space. Yoh used white ceramic tile flooring to establish a continuity between the interior and the exterior and to anchor the building to the site.

Along the natural incline of the site he created a long pathway and a set of steps that both increase the sense of spaciousness and penetrate the site from the road, through the living room, central light court, bedroom, and finally, into the garden in the rear.

Top, this drawing shows the central division of the house and the massing of the volumes on each side.
Bottom, this image shows how the "lattice" illuminates and defines the interior of the living quarters.

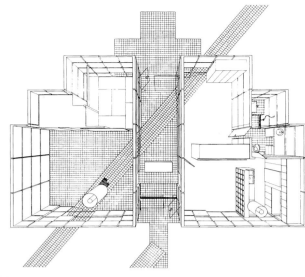

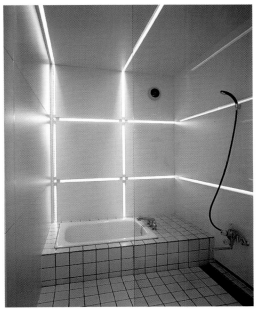

Left, the central outdoor space as seen from within the house. Above, the "lattice" is present throughout the house. Here it is seen as it defines the bathroom.

Egami Clinic

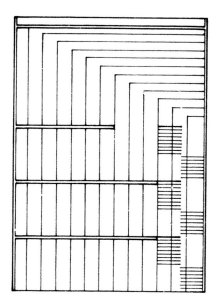

Unlike Yoh's Ingot Coffee Shop, Kinoshita Clinic, and Stainless-Steel House with Light Lattice, which sit, isolated on the landscape, his Egami Clinic, completed in 1982 in Nagasaki, is situated in a tight urban context. For this project Yoh was challenged by the idea of creating a dramatic, sculptural form like that used for the Kinoshita Clinic, while simultaneously creating a choreography of light that could be seen as a continuation of his work for the Ingot Coffee Shop and the Stainless-Steel House with Light Lattice. For this otology clinic Yoh attempted to create a form that would somehow represent sound waves, while simultaneously creating a constantly light-filled space.

Here Yoh created a zigzagging facade composed of alternating panels of glass and aluminum, the glass facing north along the street facade and then folding over to become part of the roof, so as to allow for the fullest introduction of natural light into the spaces. Throughout the various hours of the day a mellow natural light filters through the steplike screen construction and floods the space with an attractive illumination.

Like Yoh's other constructions that incorporate a play with light, the evening provides a dramatic opportunity as the forms appear to metamorphose into a gigantic accordionlike, living, breathing organism whose innards generate soft, glowing light.

Top, this plan shows the zigzagging footprint of the building and how it eventually becomes facade and roof. Center, a detail of the wall and ceiling shows how the amount of light entering the space has been maximized by the arrangement of aluminum and glass. Bottom, the form of the interior staircase reflects the program for the entire construction.

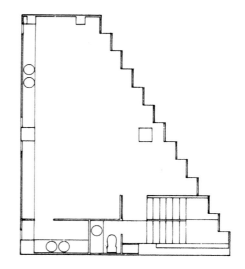

Opposite page, as seen from the street the clinic calls to mind the principals of otology.

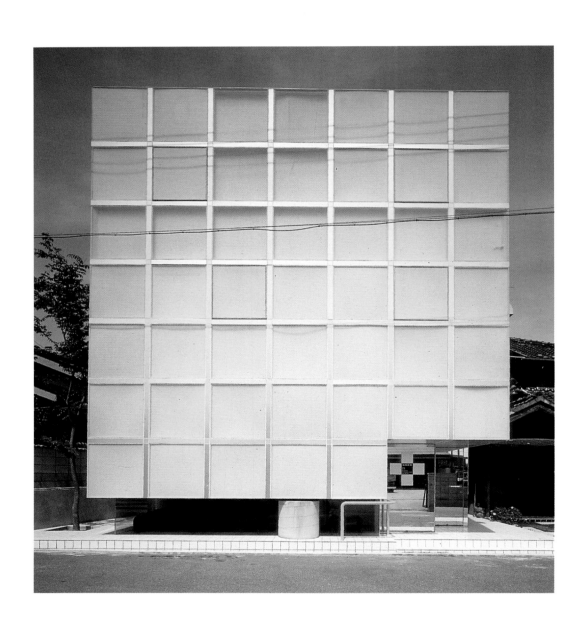

Glass House with Breathing Grating

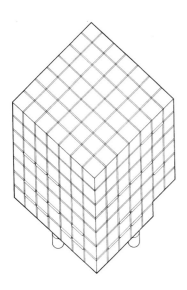

Initially, the most striking element of Yoh's Glass House with Breathing Grating is its perfectly square form. Here Yoh built an 8-meter cube and suspended it 80 centimeters above the ground to create a sense of lightness and to distinguish the building's geometry from the site. Like the Ingot Coffee Shop, this construction is covered entirely by a gridlike steel frame.

Here, in addition to the glass panels, the steel frame is capable of hosting aluminum honeycomblike gratings that may be opened for ventilation or translucent plastic panels. Yoh designed a structure that was flexible enough to permit the simple attachment or removal of the panels so that natural illumination, visibility, and ventilation could be controlled by the adjustable facade. With this project Yoh came closer to his idea of a building being able to create its own relationships to nature.

Here the framework and the various interchangeable panels create a system that appears to "breath" as it allows for ventilation, and "dilate" as it becomes more or less transparent. As the panels are alternated to relate to the natural setting the house takes on the aura of a living, breathing organism, an aura that the stark, nonorganic geometry of the structure seems to contradict.

Here Yoh introduced his ability to establish the coexistence of opposing forces—to render the geometric organic, for example, and in doing so, he initiated a diagonal dialogue with our opposing notions of nature and culture. It is this "diagonal" that allowed Yoh to open a discourse between natural phenomena and architecture.

While the construction is composed of three floors, the first for a clinic and the second and third for residential use, the exterior reads as a singular solid volume hovering above the urban site.

The flexibility of the facade seems to function independently from the division of the floors; in fact from the exterior it is virtually impossible to determine how many stories the construction contains. Yoh carried this flexibility into the floor plans where rooms are divided only as they are used for varying purposes.

This simple floor plan
illustrates how the
flexibility of traditional
Japanese residential
interiors has been
carried over to this
contemporaty setting.

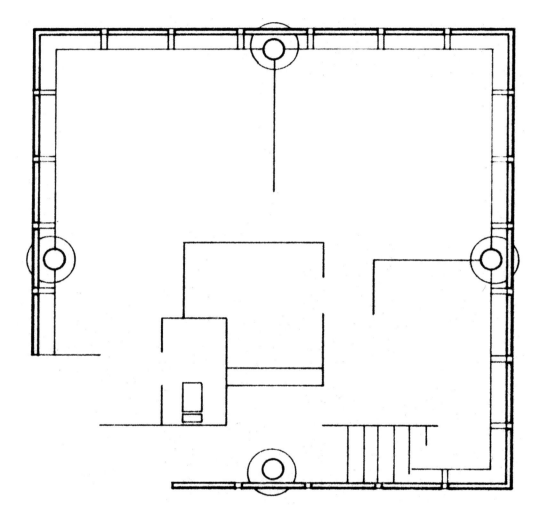

Above and below, these images of interior spaces show how the grid becomes both window and wall.

Saibu Gas Museum

The exterior of Yoh's Saibu Gas Museum for Natural Phenomenart, constructed for the Saibu Gas Co. in 1989 in Monmochi, Sawara-ku, Fukuoka-shi, Fukuoka Prefecture, looks somewhat like a power station or a gigantic machine. Here Yoh attempted to evaluate some of the most rudimentary physical phenomena through the use of some of the most advanced technologies. "The concept derives from Oriental philosophy," said Yoh of his museum, "which sets out to clarify the relationship between things rather than rely on analytical methodology." From this thought Yoh arrived at a design for the museum that placed sophisticated technology in the service of the conceptual simplicity that distinguishes natural phenomena.

In order to liberate the ground-floor plan and create a structure that seemed to float above the site, Yoh suspended the second and third floors with a series of exterior constructions and tension rods and covered the facade with reflective glass. The exterior stairs and ramps were then suspended in much the same way from structures that seem to extend out of a central core. The entire construction appears to defy the laws of gravity, and suspension is a theme that runs through the entire building. Yoh created a void or empty space at the center of the museum's interior which was designed to host the "media space" and the permanent installation of the "Machine Room." Yoh's "media space" hosts a glass floor, which calls to mind his work with glass-and-steel grids for his Ingot Coffee shop, Stainless-Steel House with Light Lattice, and Glass House with Breathing Grating. Here, once again, the glass-and-steel grid becomes the site of a spectacle of changing light effects, but here it is not the natural light of the sun or moon that is the protagonist, but rather an orchestrated performance of the cogeneration process of the machine room below. As gas is burnt to produce heat and electricity a musical score by Isao Tomita is played. Haruki Kaitoh designed the lighting to underscore the beauty of the atmosphere. Yoh incorporated a ramp that winds down towards the glass and steel surface from a set of bridges which intersect the void of his "media space." Safety and technology became the dominating programs for the design of the building, but Yoh was also interested in dispelling the illusion that mankind is able to totally control nature, and he wanted to somehow reinstate our awe and appreciation of natural phenomena while simultaneously creating a sense of unity with it. The central atrium or "media space" is surrounded by galleries that were designed to host exhibitions of art works attempting to integrate nature, science, and art while celebrating the wonders of natural gas. Yoh refers to this celebration of nature and culture as "Natural Phenomenart," and he functioned not only as the museum's architect but also as its General Producer.

This drawing illustrates
the relationship between
the various floors
and the central atrium
and its ramps.

The spectacle of changing
light as seen within the
"media space" is based
on the wonders of
natural phenomena.

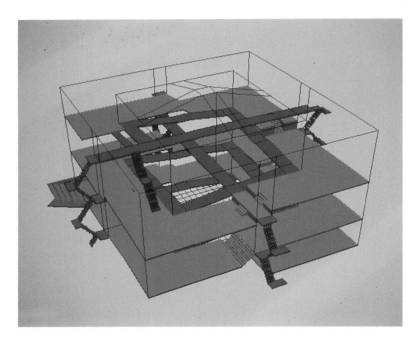

Previous page, the museum as seen from above with its exterior constructions and tension rods in full view.

Above, the exterior tension rods and constructions suspend the second and third floor above the site. The building's reflective surfacing provides an extended view of the surrounding landscape. Bottom, this drawing shows the organization of the exterior tension rods.

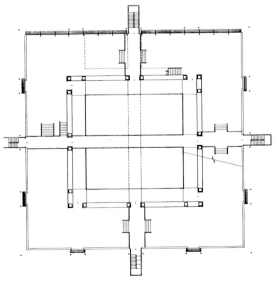

Pyramid of Sea, Ferry Terminal

Completed in 1990, Yoh's Pyramid of Sea. Ferry Terminal in Misumi, Kumamoto was part of the Artpolis Projects that were commissioned for Japan's Kumamoto Prefecture by Arata Isozaki. Isozaki was responsible for various projects throughout the area and set out to match architects to the differing public works.

In addition to Yoh, Isozaki appointed architects such as Shinohara and Renzo Piano to the highly visible and quite successful projects. The Artpolis Projects represented a challenging opportunity for all the architects and constructors involved as each of the projects became somewhat of a popular monument to the future of the area by bringing a vibrant and contemporary architectural discourse into the community.

Yoh's Pyramid of Sea is a highly visible conic form composed of a concrete structural skeleton resembling an inverted sea shell. With a base diameter of 34 meters and a height of 25 meters the ferry terminal is composed of an interior and exterior set of spiraling stairs which like the double spiraling strands of a DNA model carry visitors to an observation deck at the cone's tip.

The double spirals were used to create the structural shell of the terminal and actually stiffen the structure. Here Yoh created a building that appears to be in a state of movement, as one spirals through the structure, one encounters an array of sculpturally dynamic elements. Yoh constructed a set of fish scale-like interior stairs that appear to have grown out of the structure. Windows have also been inserted into the facade and call to mind rows of gills.

Inspired by nature, Yoh has translated that inspiration into a dynamic medley of geometric realities. Together these opposing forces create a tension that renders this structure curious and intriguing. Yoh raised the level of the ground floor to 1.5 meters above the ground and allowed for a 3 meter variable for the boarding bridge to adjust to differences in tides. The architect also installed acoustic materials under the sloping floor of the sculptural stairs/ramps and constructed an acoustic chamber under the ground floor to absorb the echo and create a stillness of sound that elevates visitors' awareness of the interior space and calls to mind the acoustic void within a sea shell.

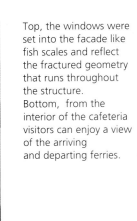

Top, the windows were set into the facade like fish scales and reflect the fractured geometry that runs throughout the structure.
Bottom, from the interior of the cafeteria visitors can enjoy a view of the arriving and departing ferries.

Opposite page, the interior calls to mind the spiraling spaces within sea shells.

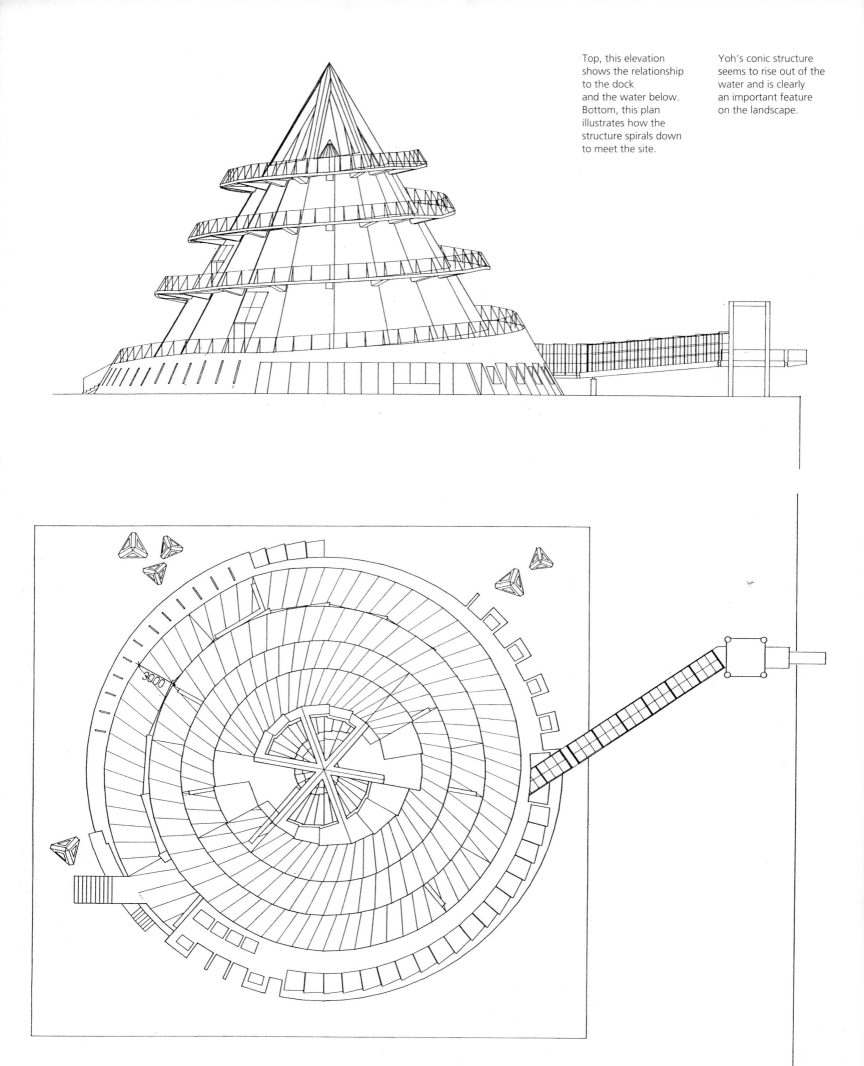

Top, this elevation shows the relationship to the dock and the water below. Bottom, this plan illustrates how the structure spirals down to meet the site.

Yoh's conic structure seems to rise out of the water and is clearly an important feature on the landscape.

Wakita Hitecs, Office

Like his Saibu Gas Museum, Yoh's Wakita Hitecs Office building completed in 1990 in Onojo, Fukuoka reveals its structures and is based on the concept of tension.

Here again exterior structures suspend the mass of the building as it appears to hover above the site.

Like a segment of a bridge, Yoh's Wakita Hitecs Office building seems to span two spaces as the structure does not stem from the materials, but from the network of forces that assure the equilibrium while creating the overall design program.

With this structure Yoh demonstrates his interest in illustrating contradictions through his architecture. His work forces us to re-think certain formal attitudes about the way in which materials create forms and how those forms are read to create a context.

Yoh has said "Being ignorant of structural theory, I have enjoyed and utilized model-making to find the rules of forces and the surprising laws of nature". Yoh's abstract models are studies of forms that have been placed within an equilibrium that renders them vital and initiates a relationship to the forces of nature. Yoh's Wakita Hitecs Office structure is free from the aestheticism often associated with high-tech architecture, his work, instead, taps into the energy that is created from his skilful manipulation of technology on one hand and the natural forces of suspension and tension on the other. Unexpectedly Yoh's building is suspended above the ground, but Yoh makes no attempt to play the part of the magician and underscores the set of cables and columns which are responsible for this suspension.

In doing so his building, like any phenomena observed in nature, illustrates exactly how it is done.

Top, this image shows
some of the detailing
of the exterior tension
structures.
Bottom, this drawing
shows how the mass
of the building is
suspended above the site.

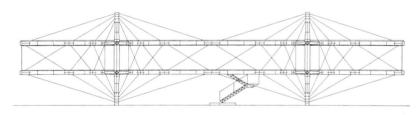

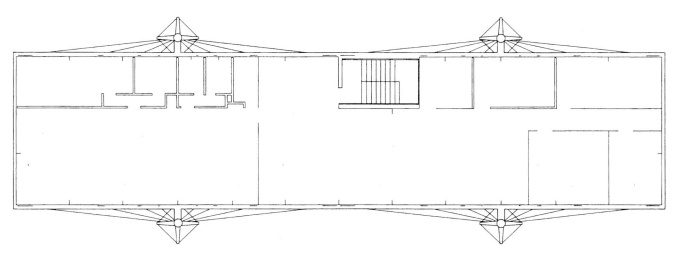

Top, this plan shows
the relationship between
the exterior structure
and the volume
of the interior spaces.
Bottom, by elevating
the mass of the
construction, Yoh
releaved the site
of the presence of an
additional construction.

Another Glass House Between Sea and Sky

In 1990 Yoh completed his Matsushita Clinic which carried the suspended forms he used in his Kinoshita Clinic and Glass House with Breathing Grating and the cantilevered forms he incorporated in his Saibu Gas Museum or Wakita Hitecs Office, for example, one step further. With Yoh's Matsushita Clinic the suspension of the structure became the focal point of the sculptural drama of the building and the architect brought the defiance of gravity into his architectural vocabulary.

The Matsushita clinic consisted of a massive concrete vertical volume extending approximately five stories above the ground. From this structure, which created a perpendicular axis with the street, Yoh suspended three shelves each one floor apart which, when seen together with their enclosures, created a receding triangular wedge of glass and steel clinic space vertiginously suspended one flight above the site. The void beneath the first suspended floor was used to create both a car port and entrance.

The following year Yoh completed his Another Glass House Between Sea and Sky which incorporated much of the same vocabulary of massive vertical volumes from which seemingly light shelf-like floors with glass enclosures were cantilevered.

With this project Yoh seems to have refined his use of cantilevered structures to the point of creating the illusion of levitation.

Yoh has described his levitating architecture as being able to create a contrast between the unstable or uncertain lightness of the structure and the heavy weight of the historical and cultural context of the site. He has created a parallel to a nomad's tent that exists temporarily on the site, not in that all his cantilevered or suspended structures are temporary like the Kinoshita Clinic, but in that they seem to exists within a precarious relationship to the site. With Another Glass House Between Sea and Sky Yoh again reveals his structures and we come to understand just how the house, or better yet the structure which suspends the house is set on a steep hill in Shima, Fukuoka 140 meters above the Japan Sea. Here I refer to the structure and the house as separate elements in that Yoh created two massive vertical wall-like anchors that stand parallel to each other and literally ground the structure to the site and support two shelf-like planes that extend well beyond the anchoring walls to form the floor and ceiling/roof of the mostly transparent house.

Yoh has also placed a narrow pool in the space between these anchoring walls at the back of the structure which further grounds the house to the site. Yoh has penetrated these structural walls with a play of step-like forms that provide the structure with the notion of simultaneously extending and returning to the earth.

Another Glass House Between Sea and Sky creates a conflict between the site and the structure and reflects this conflict in its materials. Here Yoh created a structure that is simultaneously transparent as it almost seems to blow away with the changing atmospheric conditions and firmly grounded to the site and the earth below. The result can be read as a retreat that attempts to personify the forces of nature that exist on the site. By paying homage to these forces, Yoh has created an architecture that exists within a poetic metaphor to its site.

The open interior spaces
are placed between the
shelf-like floor and roof
slabs.

This plan shows the
relationship between
the suspended interior
spaces and the
anchoring system
of two parallel walls.

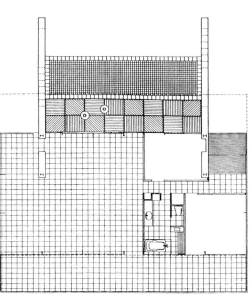

This drawing illustrates how the structure is suspended over the landscape and provides a detail of the anchoring wall.

The glass enclosed balcony shows how Yoh played with notions of transparency to maximize the dramatic effects of the site.

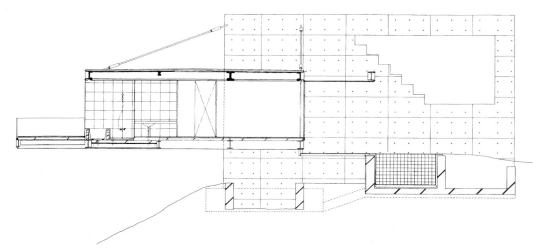

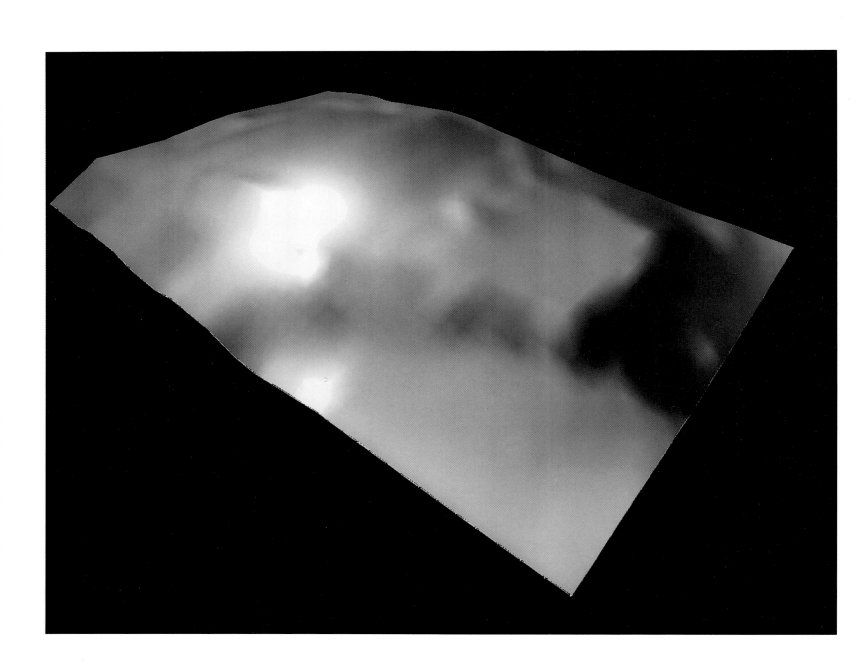

Odawara Municipal Sports Complex

Yoh designed the Oguni Dome, the largest wooden gymnasium constructed in Japan after World War II, for Oguni, a small lumber producing town near Mt. Aso, the largest active volcano in the world.

The construction was part of a larger plan of Yoh's that called for the use of three-dimensional truss structures constructed from the town's own seasoned cedar in the construction of all the new public buildings. As Japan's Building Standard restricts the use of wood, Yoh's proposal required numerous government permits and resulted in the establishment of patented construction methods. Here Yoh introduced and patented an epoxy glue filler between the wooden interface and the steel bolts and the form of the roof responded to the need to keep the wooden truss as far away from the possibility of fire on the floor as physically possible.

Yoh's Oguni Dome, which was completed in 1988, provides a foundation for understanding much of his latter work with roof structures, composed of wood, bamboo, or steel. With this project Yoh brought an idea of the organic to the form of the roof, an idea already expressed in the overall form of his Kinoshita Clinic, but developed here as a direct confrontation of modernism's abandonment of the roof as structural ornament.

Yoh's Ondawara Municipal Sports Complex in Odawara-shi in Kanagawa Prefecture was proposed in 1991 and is an example of his interest in roof structures and how an organic approach, coupled with advances created from the marriage of construction and computer technology, could inspire more fluid and open systems of construction.

Yoh has referred to the amorphous, fluttering roof structure he designed here as a giant handkerchief that simply covers the extensive athletic facilities.

Although the form initially appears to have been designed with much liberty, it was designed to simultaneously respond to specific light and sound requirements and respond to the natural mountain range and Sakawa river bank.

Yoh has also referred to this aspect of his work as aquatic architecture in that it allows for the unpredicted participation of architectural form and external forces. Yoh's design for the Odawara Municipal Sports Complex attempted to create a roof structure that would exists like an organically grown shell over the functioning of the internal components of the athletic fields as opposed to a uniform structure that would provide a mandate for the internal functions, systems, and structures.

Yoh's roof was designed to adapt not only to the different uses of the interior spaces, but to the different structural and mechanical systems within as well. With this design Yoh created a supple rather than a rigid geometry that was created with the capability of sustaining the differences within the structure in much the same way that a skin or shell exists in nature. As early as his work for his Glass House with Breathing Grating, Yoh was interested in building that would respond physically, as opposed to solely as an aesthetic mirror, to its surroundings. Yoh wanted to create buildings that contained the power of life in that they responded to natural phenomena. He believes that as technology advances it must continue to look toward nature not simply for for inspiration, but for direction as well.

The undulating Odawara roof was designed from a relatively standard grid. The main athletic fields within determined specific span lengths and ceiling heights, and a uniform snow load established the variable beam depths and roof heights.

Yoh's proposal also called for an internal surface that could be adjusted to meet varying lighting and acoustical needs. Rather than averaging these requirements into a standard dimension, Yoh maintained the differences.

These disparate forces were incorporated into a whole, flexible system designed to fluctuate in response to the needs below.

Yoh is the first to recognize that this sort of structural development is possible because new technologies can guide the design, construction, and fabrication process, but Yoh has been able to carry these technological advances back to his ideas on the natural and how it becomes the cultural.

This drawing shows how
the roof was designed
to directly address
the functions below.

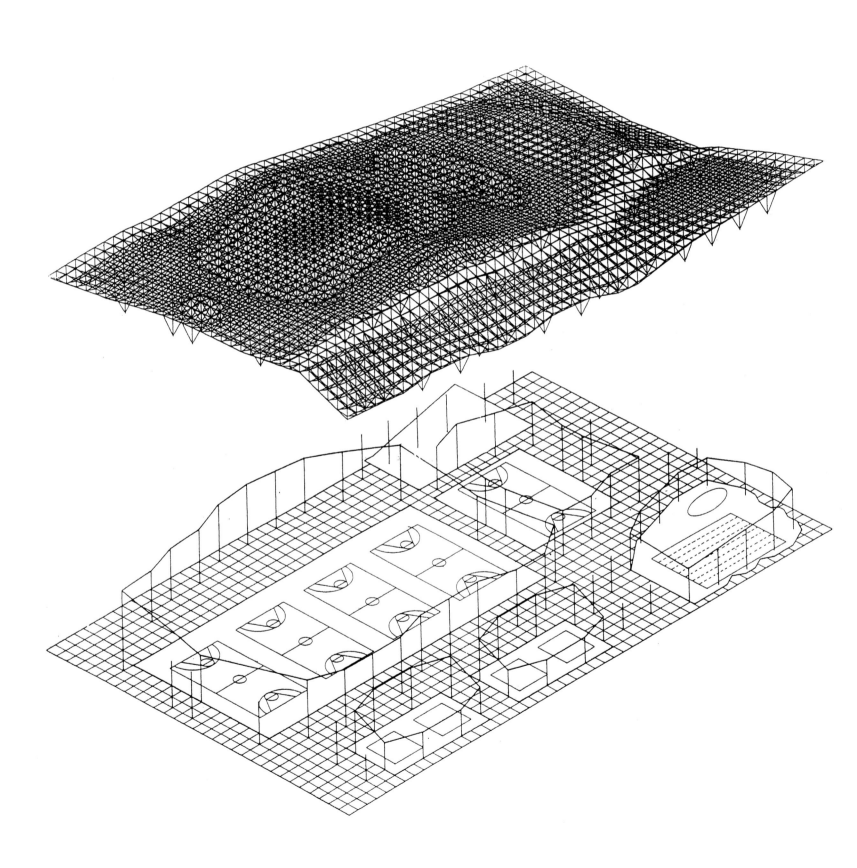

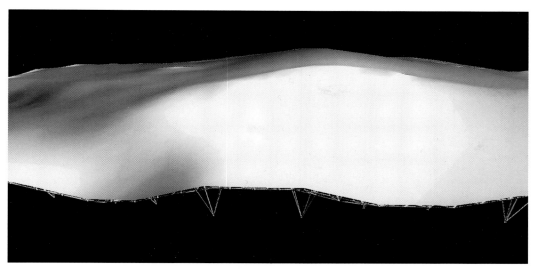

Top, this computer generated image shows the variations in the undulating roof. Bottom, this computer generated image illustrates the structural components used to support the variations in the roof.

Arashiyama Golf Club

Arashiyama Golf Club, completed in 1991, is located on a tropical hill on Okinawa Island populated by the Ryukyu Dynasty, who are famous for having maintained their traditional customs and for the coral stones their island produces. All across the island, rainwater flows over the coral, creating an effect similar to that of Italian travertine marble.

Yoh was interested in reflecting the rich heritage of this native population and in paying homage to their beautiful coral production, so he decided to incorporate a building technique known as Hinpun, which consists of the construction of a freestanding coral-stone wall in front of an entrance. This is a thoughtful device that maintains privacy while remaining welcoming to guests, but most importantly it allows cooling breezes to circulate into the space. Yoh incorporated this technique repeatedly throughout the site establishing a strong axis. Here water and waterfalls were also used to naturalize the environment, cool the air, and evoke memories of the origin of the coral.

This site plan shows the relationship the building maintains to the landscape.

Opposite page, this exterior view shows how the local coral stone was used and how it meets the landscape.

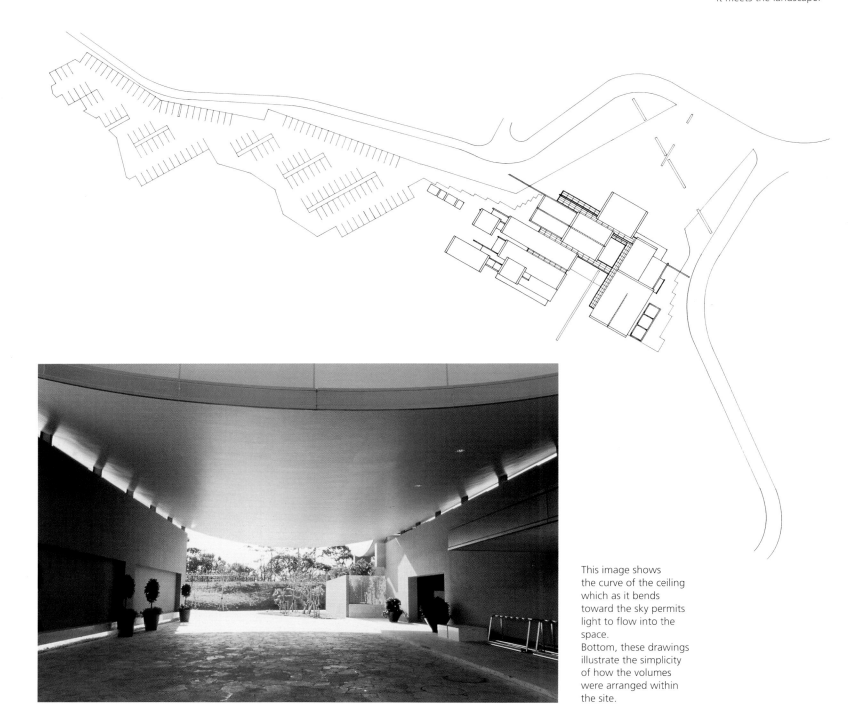

This image shows the curve of the ceiling which as it bends toward the sky permits light to flow into the space.
Bottom, these drawings illustrate the simplicity of how the volumes were arranged within the site.

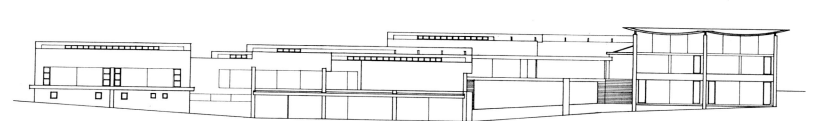

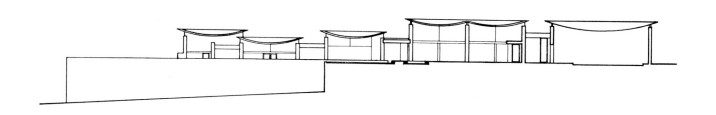

Yokohama Daikou Pier Aerial City, 2050

In 1992, as part of the Yokohama Urban Ring Exhibition, Yoh proposed an urban high-rise city for the year 2050 that would maximize the ecological use of the land. The chosen site was to lie at the juncture of the three cities of Kawasaki, Yokohama, and Tokyo and provide access to the Chiba Prefecture as well. Yoh's plan would link together the Yokohama Bay Bridge, the Daikoku Pier, and Haneda Airport with a network of suspended, three-dimensional roads. The plan was based on a desire to liberate the ground from traffic and congestion and to embrace a notion of city planning that could abandon the standard horizontal grid and its corresponding coordinates in vertical partitions and perpendicular connections.

Yoh's proposal attempted to create a truly three-dimensional urban space formed by a freedom of movement. The Yokohama Daikoku Pier, Aerial City, 2050 proposal called for the provision of an urban setting with systems that were inspired by the natural and the organic, as opposed to the static geometric use of the ground.

Yoh's proposal called for the construction of Le Grand Cube office building which was to be as large as Le Grand Arche in Paris and lie on the same axis as the Champs Elysées, this cubelike structure would be accessible from an elevated high-way. A star-shaped yacht club in the form of Kepler's octagon was planned to stand directly on Yokohama Harbor and provide recreational and transportation access to the water, and the Trident Cross, a high-rise complex, composed of three towers leaning into each other to form a tripodlike structure allowing for communication between and access to the different towers at their intersection high above the ground; the Hotel Dimaryp which is an inverted replica of the form of King Cheops' pyramid found in Gizeh, Egypt; and the Unité d'habitation, Yokohama, a Le Corbusier–inspired residential building created conceptually from the potential of placing all four of Le Corbusier's Unité d'habitation in Marseille into a spiraling tower.

The lower parts of each of Yoh's super-high-rise-buildings included in this proposal are open to allow for pedestrian and recreational activities. To restore and conserve the natural environment, the roads have all been removed from the ground and placed in the air.

Yoh's proposal called for an urban environment with ramplike roads reaching elevations of over 100 meters which would free the environment of grids of traffic at ground level. One would enter the buildings in Yoh's Aerial City through the traditional entrance hall or lobby, but here it would become a node functioning like the concourse of a railway station suspended high above the ground.

From these nodes, people would move freely to the upper and lower floors. Here private residences and hotels would be linked directly from door to door by a double spiral, similar to the one used in the 1991 Pyramid of the Sea project.

Yoh's proposal aimed to remove all the roads, streets, and traffic lights from the ground and give the earth back to the natural environment. In this futuristic vision of cities linked together by light, ribbonlike skyways the asphalt jungle would become a thing of the past and urban planning would leave the two dimensions of street maps and floor plans to enter into the space already occupied by all natural phenomena.

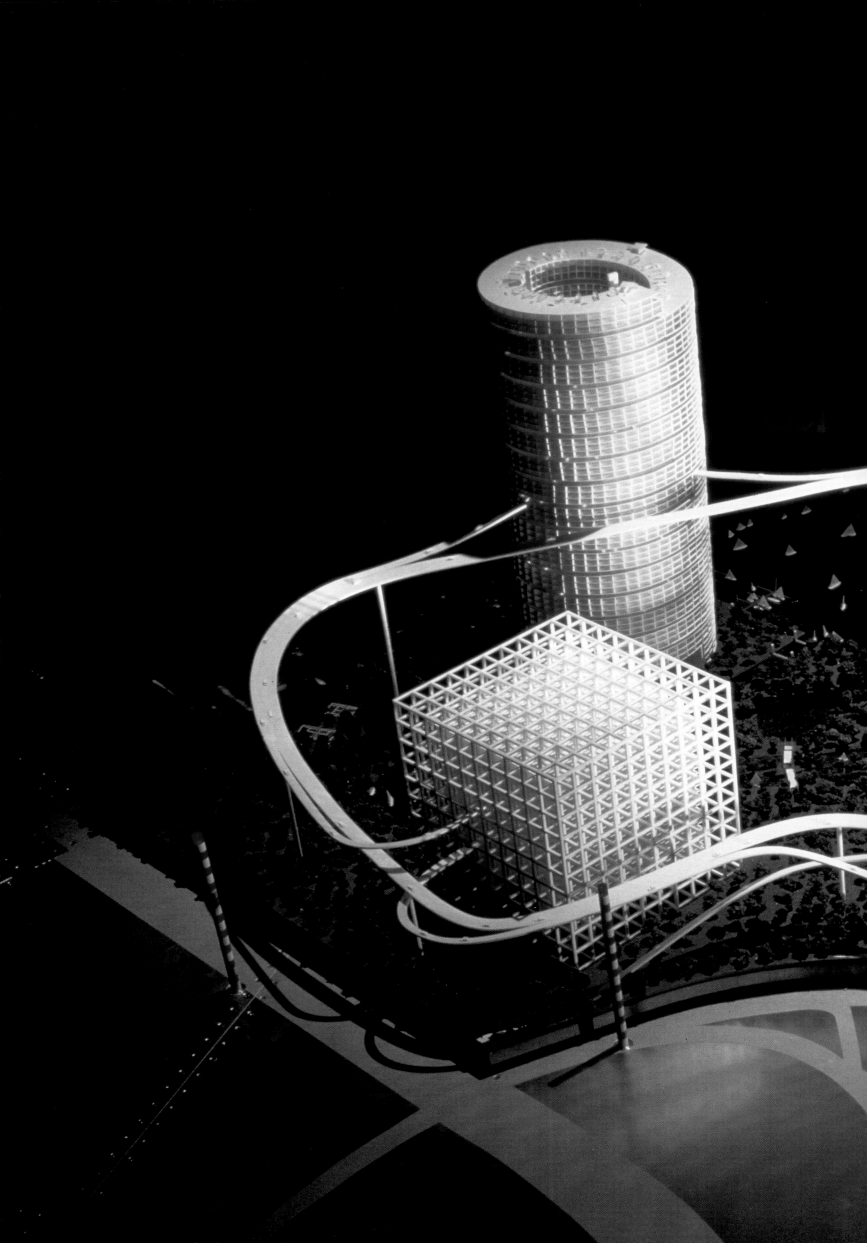

Prospecta '92 Toyama, Observatory Tower

Yoh completed his Prospecta '92 Toyama, Observatory Tower in Kosugi, Toyama in 1992. The imposing 30-by-32-by-32-meter observation tower was conceived as a midair museum dedicated to the beauty of the earth and universe.

The project was called Prospecta '92 in honor of the beautiful scenery that is revealed from the 31.8-meter height of the observation deck that sits on top of a 61.2-meter hill. The massive framelike structure set within the landscape is composed of twelve 5-by-5-meter structural beams and pillars, with four vertical members housing two elevators and two stairways. With this project Yoh set out to create a simple structure that would provide visitors with the opportunity to contemplate the natural beauty of the nearby snow-covered mountains, while at the same time he wanted to create a dramatic contrast to the natural environment. Here, as with his Another Glass House Between Sea and Sky, for example, Yoh incorporated the strategy of emphasizing the differences between nature and culture, between the environment and the constructed, in order to heighten awareness of nature and natural phenomena.

Yoh's concept for this site seems to have taken inspiration from his 1989 Media Space at the Saibu Gas Museum in Fukuoka Prefecture. For this project Yoh used points overlooking the central atrium or void within the Museum to provide a view of the Machine Room, where the conversion of natural gas into other forms of energy becomes a spectacle accompanied by choreographed lighting and sound.

Prospecta '92 Toyama, Observatory Tower may be called an open-air theater similar to Yoh's Media Space, but here the spectacle of natural gas has been replaced by an orchestrated performance of fog, light, music, and sound that changes as the atmospheric conditions of the site change. As one of the themes of the observation tower is the cycle of Toyama's cherished water, in the void or courtyard there is a fog-generating apparatus that creates tiny drops of water, which eventually gather to create a small stream flowing into a waterfall and eventually pouring into the sea. Working on these special effects with Yoh were Masao Nihei, who designed the lighting, and Fujiko Nakaya who designed the fog effects, while the music was assembled by Senji Mori.

The spectacle of observation, as presented here by Yoh, can be enjoyed from one of the two levels corresponding to the eight sides of the framelike cube structure that are parallel to the ground, from four open walkways at the base of the building, and four glass-enclosed corridorlike observation areas above. With his work with natural phenomenon, Yoh attempts to create one entity from fundamentally different elements. He attempts to create an integrated site, place, or even city from our capacity to simultaneously divide and join, to attach and isolate. His idea for Prospecta '92 Toyama, Observatory Tower attempts to be both site-specific and global in his desire to embrace a notion of nature in his architecture.

This drawing illustrates
how the elevator and
stair banks carry visitors
to the upper level.

Opposite page, the tower
as seen in the mist-filled
landscape.

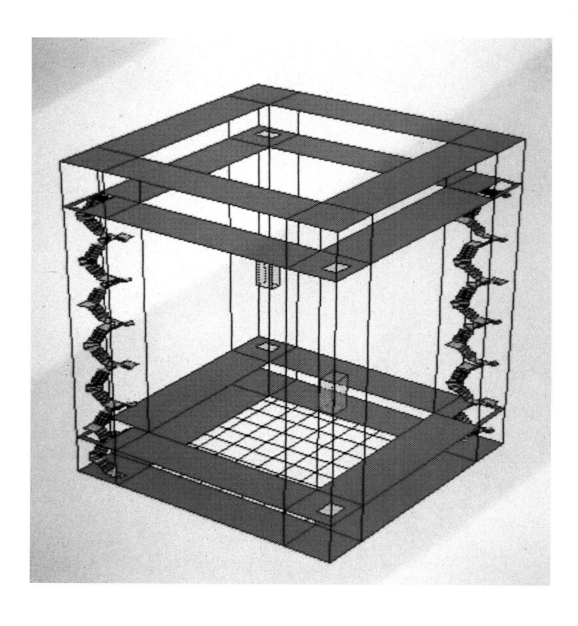

The entrance to the
exhibition space
on the upper level,
and the interior of the
exhibition space

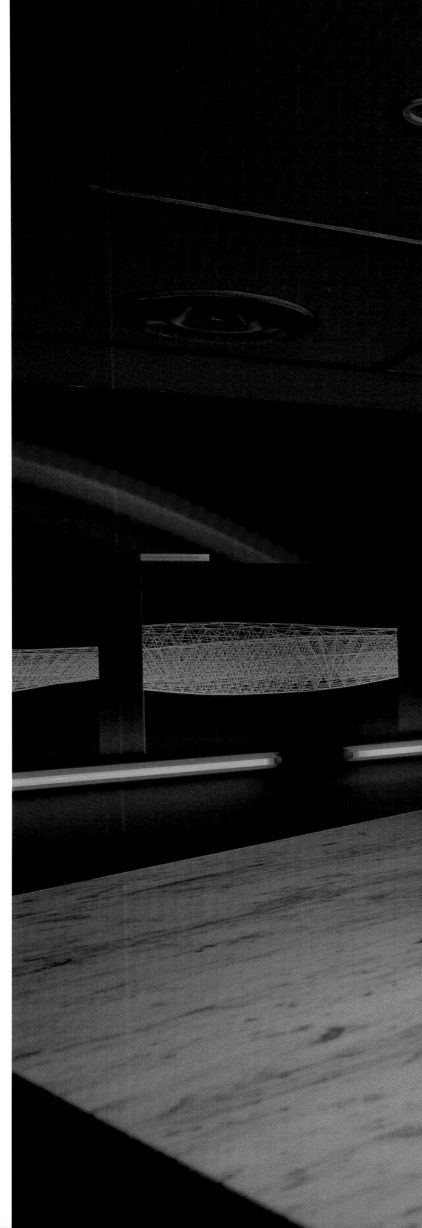

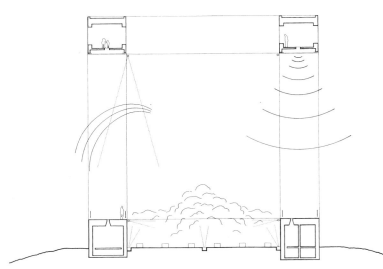

Top, this drawing
indicates how the audio
and mist-effects travel
throughout the space.
Bottom, visitors enjoy
the spectacle of changing
atmospheric conditions.

A detailed view of the
light and mist effects

The tower as seen on the landscape.
Bottom, the view back onto the structure from the observation deck.

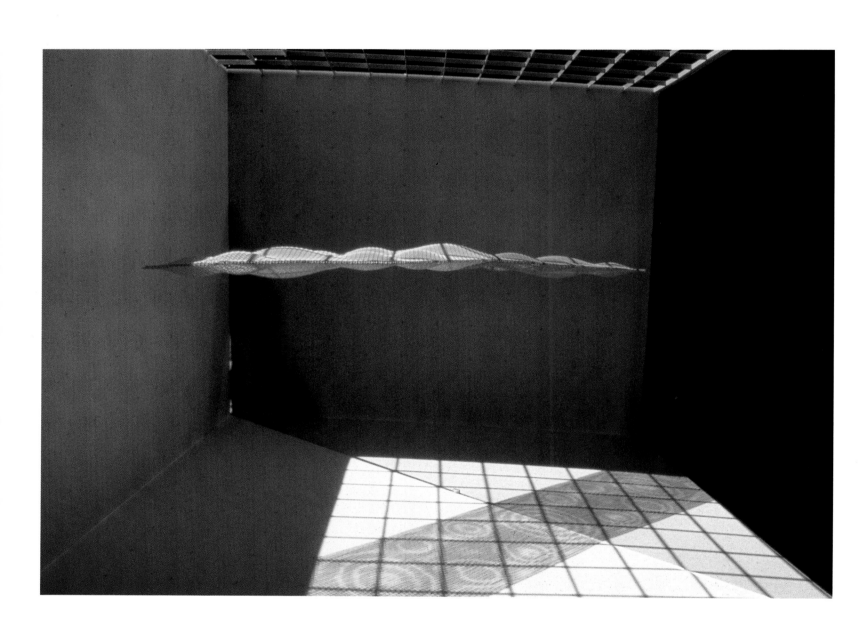

Galaxy Toyama 1992, Gymnasium

A roof is defined as the exterior upper covering of a building—perhaps the most basic structure of all. With his work on the roof of his Odawara Municipal Sports Complex, Yoh attempted to respond to the internal conditions of the structure and in this sense the roof became a quasi-organic skin or shell for the building.

For his Galaxy Toyama 1992, Gymnasium in Kosugi, Toyama, Yoh's intervention might be seen as the creation of a suspended, mechanical landscape hovering over his structure. The roof here is neither still or moving, as it conveys the impression of transient natural phenomena such as cloud formations, snowdrifts, or sand dunes. It becomes an metaphysical expression leading the eye from its expansive representation of the earth to the mountains and sky beyond. The roof here functions as a reminder that the construction itself now belongs to the environment, as it attempts to create its own harmony with its surroundings.

Yoh arrived at the form of the Galaxy Toyama 1992, Gymnasium roof by calculating the transformations in the shape of the roof under a heavy load of winter snow, and he altered the thickness of the structural trusses to respond to these conditions. The result is a shape that resembles a floating cloud in the sky, and, as one enters the space, one has the impression of being within a complex galaxy. It was from this experience that Yoh generated the project's name. He wanted to connect his construction to the Crystal Palace, which was constructed for the first world exposition in London.

He believes that as the Crystal Palace anticipated the industrial age of glass and steel, his Galaxy Toyama 1992, Gymnasium, with its cloudlike roof, will usher in an age of computer technology that will enable the imitation and re-creation of natural phenomenon. Yoh placed his construction on an axis of 25,8 degrees westward, tying the construction to the 1850 Expo in London. The angle formed by the two axes can be interpreted as the angle between the histories of earth and man.

This computer
generated image
illustrates how
the various structural
supports had to respond
to the differing roof
requirements.

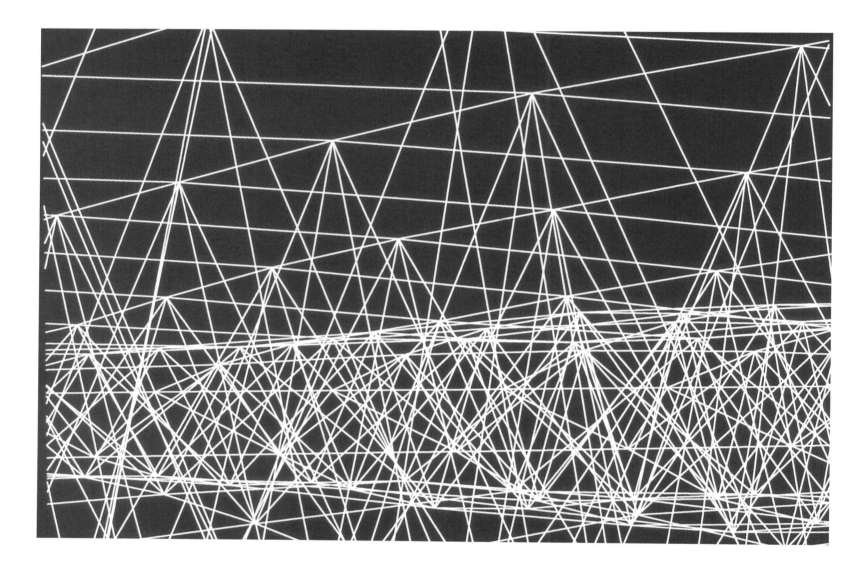

Left, this drawing shows the detail of one of the roof comumns.

Right, top, this computer generated image shows the complexity of the roof structure; bottom, this computer generated image shows the diversity of the roofing surface structure.

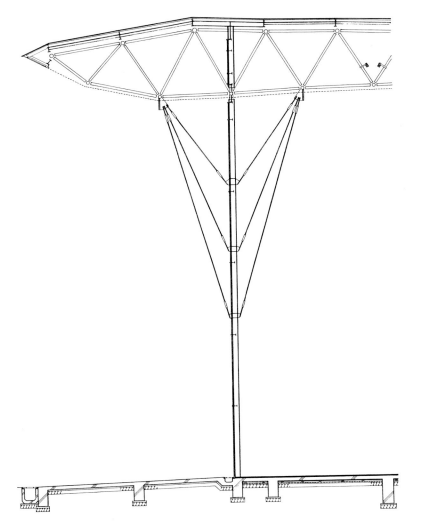

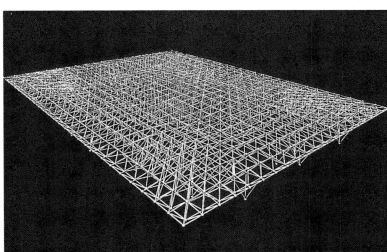

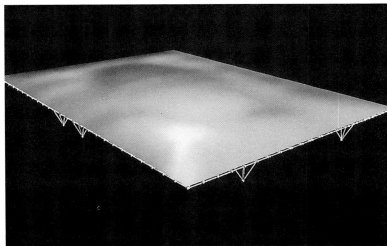

The interior space has become a celebration of the roof's architecture.

This view of the exterior
illustrates the balance
between the complexity
of the structure
and the transparency
of the glass walls.
Here the suspended roof
seems to become
a continuation of the
landscape.

Previous page, the ramps and staircases within the space reflect the design program of the structural roof supports.

The exterior glass walls reflect the surrounding landscape by day.

Opposite page, in the evening the interior of the space glows with light to expose the grid of the glass walls and the tension rods supporting the structure.

Glass Station

Like a gigantic soap bubble or a bending tennis racket, Yoh's undulating laminated glass canopy covers a gas station situated at the entrance to the small lumber-producing town of Oguni, near Mt. Aso. This glass-and-concrete structure, completed in 1993, can be seen as a not-too-distant relative of Yoh's Oguni Dome, which was constructed in the same town some five years earlier. Viewing both of the structures allows us to understand how Yoh's work with roof structures has developed into a complex mixture of natural inspiration, technological advancements, and an acute interest in challenging the capabilities of materials and mixtures of materials.

For the Glass Station he used a mixture of glass, stainless steel, polyester film, aluminum channels, structural silicone, perforated stainless-steel sheeting, and concrete, in order to construct his strikingly amorphous, parabola-shaped canopy and simultaneously meet local safety ordinances mandating a completely fire-resistant structure. The Benedictus award jury observed in 1994 that the glass is "ideal in its capacity to apparently stretch and maintain its shape over the parabolic planes of the canopy."

Four poured-in-place concrete arches, each of different heights and depths, were set along the edges of the wedge-shaped site, and a lattice grid of 22-millimeter diameter, pretensioned steel rods and aluminum channels was stretched between the arches like the strings of a tennis racket, then bolted to the concrete structures. The rods and channels created the parabolic, curved frame into which the glass and perforated stainless steel was precisely cut to fit into the varying spaces of this metal grid. Each of the panels was then mounted to the top flange of the aluminum channels and fastened with structural silicone joints. Yoh not only incorporated this sort of flexible joint on many of his previous projects that incorporated glass, steel, and aluminum lattice, but he introduced and developed this technique because of its ability to absorb the movement caused by thermal changes.

Yoh used a combination of 8-millimeter-thick laminated glass and a 0.3-millimeter-thick sheet of perforated stainless steel to filter the sunlight below the canopy. A polyester film was also placed between the glass roofing and the metal support structure to provide additional safety in the case of any broken glass.

Top and bottom, these computer generated images illustrate the relationship between the four points where the roof meets the ground and the form of the bubble-like roof.

Glass Station, a view of under the roof shows how the beautifully complex structure shelters a simple filling station.

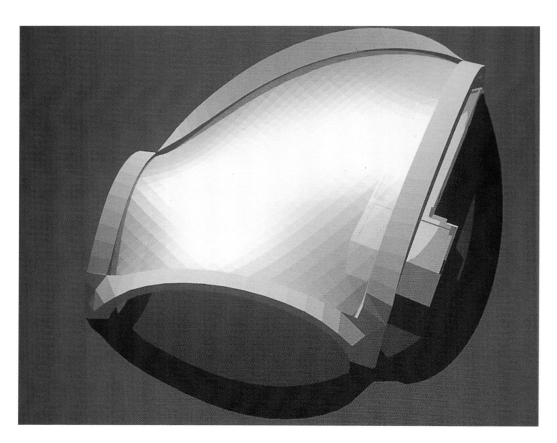

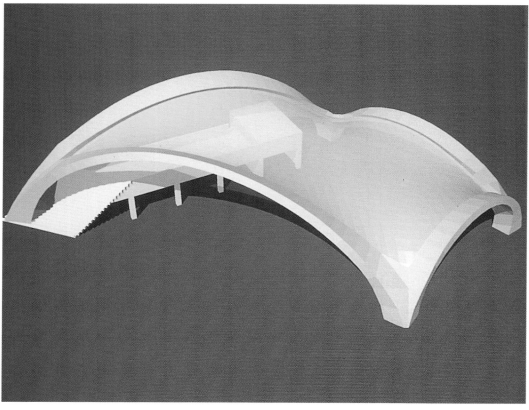

This detail shows how the various glass panels were fitted into the undulating structure.

As seen from above the glass and concrete structure seems to blend with the gently sloping hills in the background.

Kanada Children Training House

Yoh's constructions stimulate the imagination and create a respect for natural phenomena. With this in mind, it becomes clear that children would benefit greatly from a direct experience with his architecture. The Kanada Children Training House, completed in 1994 on a hillside in Kanada, Fukuoka is composed of four triangular prism-shaped constructions that are cantilevered from their anchor within the landscape to extend 12 meters into the void created by the downward sloping terrain.

The triangular wooden structures initially call to mind forms of primitive housing, but upon further examination one comes to wonder about the technology that suspends the structures without the use of posts or columns. In addition to the dramatic suspension of the structure, Yoh has opened the most structurally critical corners of the triangular forms for light, air, and a fragmented view similar to the experience he created in his Stainless-Steel House with Light Lattice in 1980.

Here Yoh relies on the contrast created between the undulating natural green field and the geometric composition of the structures, and this contrast calls to mind his 1977 project, the Ingot Coffee Shop, a glass-and-lattice-framed, prismlike form set within a parklike setting. Yoh has used geometry to underline natural phenomena, and he believes that geometry can serve as a simple tool for the appreciation of nature. His work illustrates that the use of cubes, spheres, cones, and pyramids, for example, does not require the application of high technology, but rather a clarity of thought and philosophy of application.

While it is his use of irregular forms that directly responding to nature that requires the high technology of computer simulation and highly advanced systems of fabrication and manufacture, Yoh's work with simple geometry in relation to natural settings empowers man and strengthens his relationship to nature—a fitting scenario for an educational facility for children.

The various triangular
elements of this training
House are each curiously
suspended over the
landscape.

Top, this section
illustrates
the relationship the
structures maintain
to the sloping ground.
Bottom, this site shows
how the various
constructions are united
and how they relate
to the landscape.

110

Naiju Community Center and Nursery School

In much of Yoh's work grids become a means of organizing the space, whether those grids are transformed into a Light Lattice, Breathing Grating, or are developed to create complex structures capable of responding to curvilinear programs. For Yoh, the development of this most basic geometric arrangement of horizontal and vertical coordinates has become a means of maintaining a philosophy of simplicity even in his most complex structures.

He is also fond of revealing his secrets, or, as here, his structures. We are never in awe of the physical, technological, or mechanical advancements of one of his buildings without being allowed access to an understanding of how it was constructed, and that construction, no matter how complex or innovative, is always grounded in rather simple principles of construction.

For the Naiju Community Center and Nursery School, completed in the small town of Chikuho, Fukuka, in 1994, Yoh was faced with the challenge of creating a structure that would somehow bring the community together and function as a monument to the place and its people.

Yoh's Oguni Dome project, completed in 1988, was highly successful in that it created an innovative structure by pushing the limits of the locally produced cedar. In order to do so, Yoh had to file for various government permits and develop new technologies for his

use of the wood. The final project, however, represents a coming-together of various elements, not simply his architectural intervention, but a notion of civic pride and the construction of a building that truly reflected its site in an organic manner. For the Naiju Community Center and Nursery School Yoh became inspired by the local canned-bamboo factories and decided to use the material for the structure. As bamboo is not an officially recognized building material in Japan, again special government permission was required, in addition to various studies on the structural capacities of the material.

In addition to his plan to use local materials, Yoh had hoped that the community center would, at least in part, be built with community participation, and this required that the construction process be kept simple. Members of Yoh's design team worked together with local craftsman to literally weave a complex bamboo grid like a gigantic expanse of chair caning.

The flat structure was then suspended from a temporary post and stretched over the site in much the same way that a tent might be raised.

The bamboo structure became pliant and netlike, and, with the aid of a barn fire set within the open structure, the team of architects, contractors and community members were able to bend the bamboo into the necessary form. The undulating, cagelike form was

then covered with steel mesh and concrete. A temporary post was removed in four weeks. The smooth forms of Yoh's Naiju Community Center and Nursery School sit within the landscape like a gigantic, inverted flower.

The structure attempts to internalize the cultural and contextual forces within its forms. Here Yoh has united disparate elements—local craftsmanship with advanced technology, bamboo with poured concrete—in order to create a bending, folding, and undulating form that reflects the cultural position of the community and functions as a monument to their lives and work.

This drawing illustrates
the simplicity
of the interior spaces.

Here the undulating roof
simply lifts up to create
an entrance
at ground level.

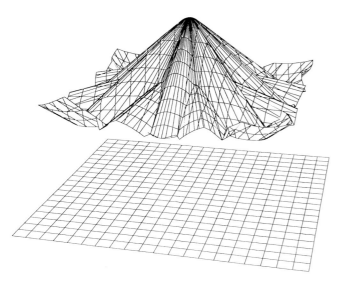

These computer generated images illustrate how the standard grid has been manipulated to form the cone-like structure.

This view shows how the roof has become a sculptural element on the landscape.

Uchino Community Center for Seniors and Children

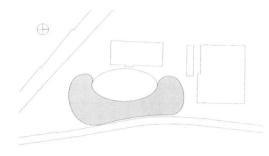

After the success, both structurally and on the level of community response, of Yoh's Naiju Community Center and Nursery School, the architect created a second bamboo-and-concrete structure for the same community of Chikuho, Fukuoka. This second structure, the Uchino Community Center for Seniors and Children, completed in 1995, needed to accommodate both senior citizens and children in a multipurpose facility that would create a bridge between the two generationally diverse groups, promoting communication and educational exchange.

With the exception of the private living quarters, here Yoh created a partition-free space that flows organically between another building to establish an oval-shaped lawn plaza creating a semi-closed courtyard garden between the new curvilinear form and the existing rectangular building.

In contrast to the flat surface of the floor, the building hosts a variety of ceiling heights that appear to be irregular and haphazard but in reality have been logically derived from structural calculations in which the ceiling height was modified in proportion to the distance between pairs of opposing columns.

As in the Naiju Community Center and Nursery School, a bamboo grid or lattice was constructed and then deformed into a three-dimensionally curved surface to become the frame of the roof. The bamboo structure was then used as a form upon which the concrete was cast.

After having withstood the tension of the deformation and the weight of the concrete pour, the bamboo lattice was left as an interior finish and testimony to both the bamboo-producing community and the construction of the building.

These computer generated images illustrate the movement within the grid pattern used to construct the roof.

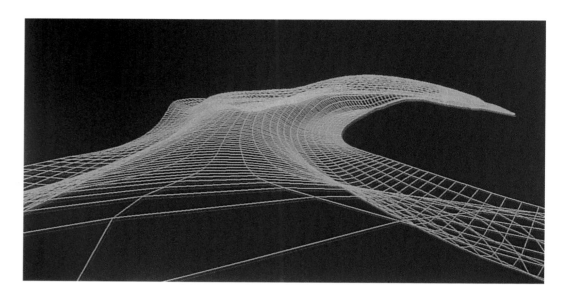

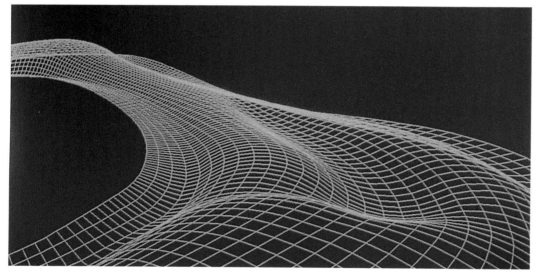

This computer generated image illustrates the relationship between the walls and the structural pattern of the grid used.

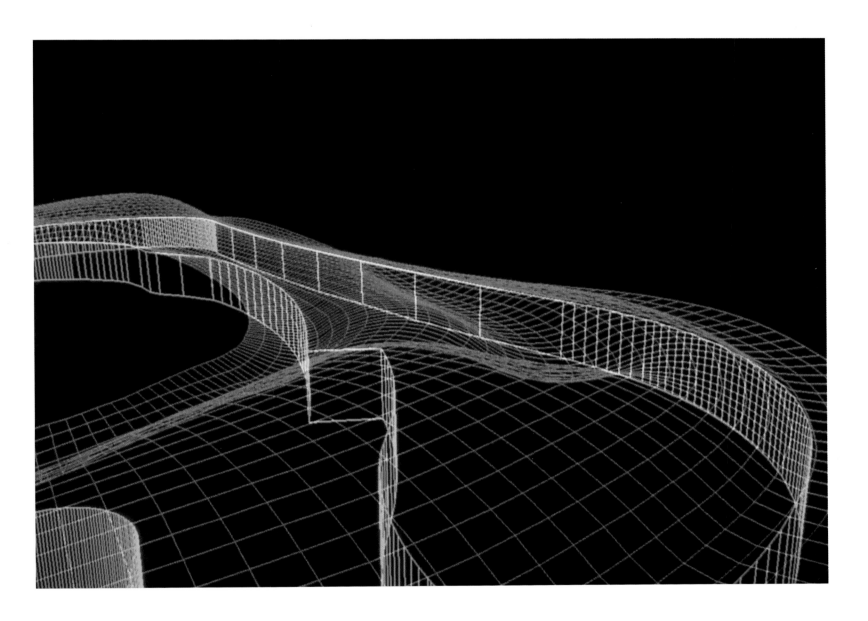

This view of the
undulating roof, as seen
from above, illustrates
how the curved building
creates an interior
courtyard.

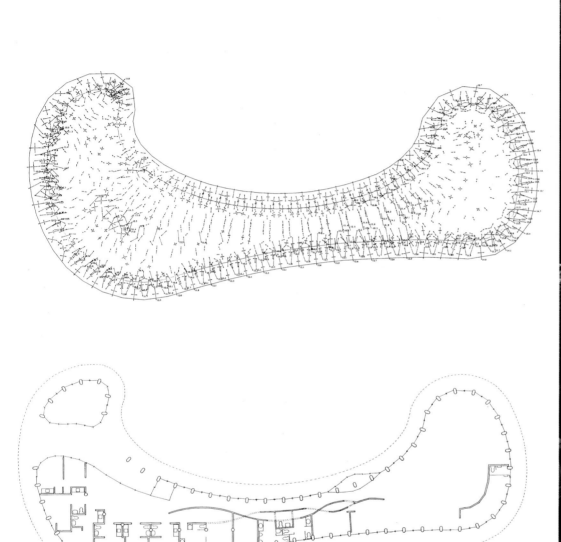

This interior view of the dining facility illustrates how the structure of the roof construction has become an important design element.

This interior view during
the final stages of
construction reveals the
importance of the roof
structure as it directs
sight lines through
the spaces.

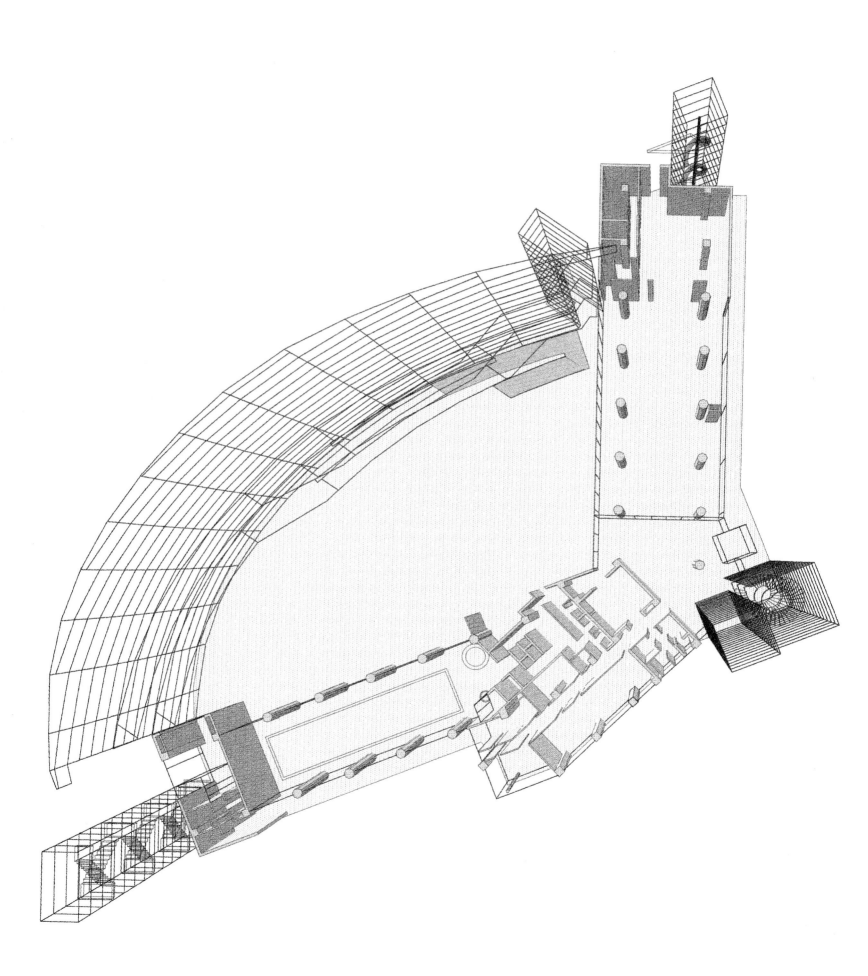

Sundial House II

In 1984 Yoh completed his Sundial House, a composition of two aluminum-clad, quarter-cylinder blocks built with techniques similar to those he developed some four years earlier for his Stainless-Steel House with Light Lattice. The facade of Yoh's Sundial House, like the Stainless-Steel House with Light Lattice, was perforated with slits of glass along the coordinates of the grid structure.

As the sun moved throughout the day its rays would directly enter one set of the perforations about every hour, casting dramatic lighting effects within and functioning as a sort of sundial. When Yoh was faced with the challenge of designing a nursing home for 100 senior citizens on the adjacent site, his thoughts returned to his earlier project.

Managed and operated by the Horikawa Hospital, Yoh's Sundial House II exceeds the government standards for nursing homes, as it responds directly to the individual residents' needs, and desire for privacy, while also offering community space that goes beyond the standard common room often found in such establishments.

Yoh brought to this project his interest in nature and his ability to create vital relationships to the natural surroundings within enclosed spaces. For this project Yoh duplicated the southern-facing curved wall of his Sundial House, but here nestled it between the two wings of the facility which open to a 112.5-degree angle. Within this opening Yoh created a large light-filled atrium from a curving and bowing exterior wall and roof skin of glass and structural steel.

Yoh gave the glass this three-dimensionality in order to properly resist wind and snow. The atrium created from this transparent structure became the center of the facility and functioned like an urban square, equipped with a restaurant, cafe, swimming pool, barber shop, vending machines, athletic gym, bulletin boards, and a nursery school, all located around the space. The atrium of Yoh's Sundial House II provides a feeling of being enclosed and exposed to nature at the same time: the outside was brought inside and the entire structure appears to be almost turned inside-out.

Yoh named this project after his previous work on the nearby site and after the residents, who are all sundials themselves.

Previous page, the entry way here reflects the design program which is expanded and continued within.

The enclosed stairways have become architectural elements that indicate the movement of the various elements.

Opposite page, this view
of the exterior illustrates
how the curving facade
is in actualtiy
a combination
of manipulated grid
structures.

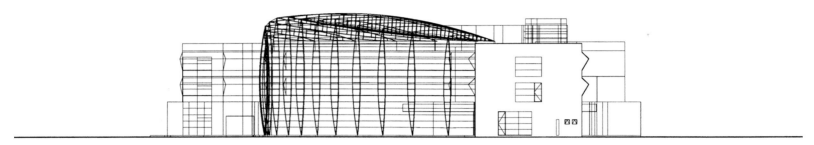

EAST ELEVATION

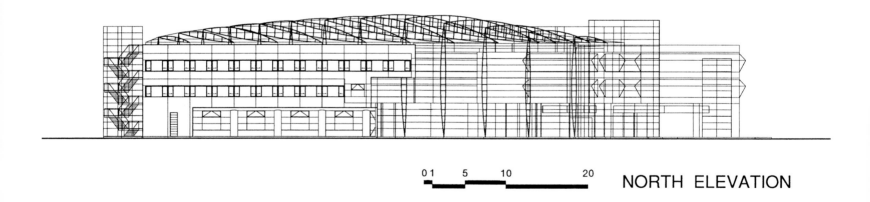

0 1   5   10   20   NORTH ELEVATION

Previous page,
the interiors reflect the
notions of transpariency
that here attempt to
document the various
stages of the moving
sun.

Left, this drawing shows
how the tow masses
open to create
an interior atrium.
Right,the interiors were
designed to transform
the sunlight into an
architectural element.

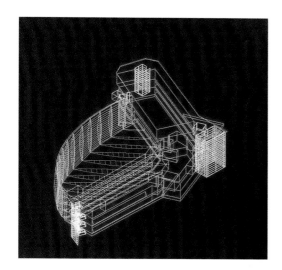

The hallways open onto the light-filled central atrium where the movement of the sun has become part of the design program.

List of works

Ingot Coffee Shop 1977,
Kitakyushu, Japan
Shoei Yoh Architects

Kinoshita Clinic 1979,
Nishi-ku, Fukuoka-shi,
Fukuoka Prefecture, Japan
Shoei Yoh Architects
Tokunaga Sekkei Jimusho
Sanken Setsubi Sekkei Jimusho
Constructed by Fukushima Komuten

Stainless-Steel House with Light Lattice
1977, Nagasaki, Japan
Shoei Yoh Architects

Egami Clinic 1982, Nagasaki, Japan
Shoei Yoh Architects

Glass House with Breathing Grating
1983, Ube, Japan
Shoei Yoh Architects
Fukuokachuoh Kosho
Constructed by Imada Komuten

Saibu Gas Museum 1989,
Monmochi, Sawara-ku, Fukuoka-shi,
Fukuoka Prefecture, Japan
Kasaba Structural Design
Takenaka Komuten
Constructed by Tekenaka Komuten

Pyramid of the Sea, Ferry Terminal 1990,
Misumi, Kumamoto, Japan
Shoei Yoh Architects
Kusaba Structural Design
Sin-Nihon Setsubi Keikaku Co., Ltd.
Constructed by Iwanaga-gumi Co., Ltd.

Wakita Hitecs Office 1990,
Onojo, Fukuoka, Japan
Shoei Yoh Architects
Kusaba Structural Design
Ariyoshi Mechanical Engineers
Constructed by Ando Kensetsu

Another Glass House Between
Sea and Sky 1991,
Shima, Fukuoka, Japan
Shoei Yoh Architects
Kusaba Structural Design
Ariyoshi Mechanical Engineers
Constructed by Fukushima Komuten
and AIRS

Odawara Municipal Sports Complex
1991,
Odawara-shi, Kanagawa Prefecture, Japan
Shoei Yoh Architects

Kusaba Structural Design
Taiyo Kogyo Corporation
Shin-Nihon Setsubi Keikaku

Arashiyama Golf Club 1991,
Okinawa, Japan
Shoei You Architects
Kusaba Structural Design

Yokohama Daikou Pier, Aerial City, 2050
1992,
Yokohama Urban Ring Exhibition
Proposal
Shoei Yoh Architects

Prospecta '92 Toyama, Observatory
Tower 1992,
Kosugi, Toyama, Japan
Shoei Yoh Architects
Kusaba Structural Design
Toyama Prefecture
Constructed by Terasaki Kogyo,
Matsushima Kogyo, and Marutaka
Kensetsu

Galaxy Toyama 1992, Gymnasium 1992,
Kosugi, Toyama, Japan
Shoei Yoh Architects
Kusaba Structural Design
Toyama Prefecture
Taiyo Kogyo Corporation
Constructed by Taisei, Kawada Kogyo,
Nisso Kensetsu

Glass Station 1993,
Oguni, Aso, Kumamoto, Japan
Shoei Yoh Architects
Kusaba Structural Design
Taiyo Kogyo Corporation
Ariyoshi Mechanical Engineers
Constructed by Ando Kensetsu
and Glass House between sea and sky

Kanada Children's Training House
1994, Kanada, Fukuoka, Japan
Shoei Yoh Architects
Kusaba Structural Design
Ariyoshi Mechanical Engineers
Kaneko Mechanical Engineers
Constructed by Kuwano-gumi
and Yuki-gumi

Naiju Community Center and Nursery
School 1994,
Chikuho, Fukuoka, Japan
Shoei Yoh Architects
Kusaba Structural Design
Gengo Matsui

Yoichi Minagawa
Ariyoshi Mechanical Engineers
Fujino Electrical Engineers
Constructed by Koh Juken

Uchino Community Center for Seniors
and Children 1995,
Chikuho, Fukuoka, Japan
Shoei Yoh Architects
Ikuo Tokuhiro
Kusaba Structural Design
Ariyoshi Mechanical Engineers
Fujino Electrical Engineers
Constructed by Hazama Corporation

Sundial House II 1996,
Kurume, Fukuoka, Japan
Shoei Yoh Architects
Kusaba Structural Design
Ariyoshi Mechanical Engineers
Ueda Electrical Engineers
Constructed by Taisei Kensetsu

Biography

Shoei Yoh was born in Kumamoto, Japan in 1940. He graduated from the Department of Economics, Keio Gijuku University, Tokyo in 1962. Studying on a foreign student grant, he majored in Fine and Applied Arts at Wittenberg University, Springfield, Ohio. In 1970 he established Yoh Design Office. Yoh has been awarded various awards including: Japan Interior Designers Association Award, 1979; Japan Architectural Association Award for Stainless-Steel House with Light Lattice, 1980; Mainichi Design Award, 1983; Kumamoto City Award for Excellence in Architecture for Pavilion retail center, 1984; Commercial Space Design Award for the La Foret Museum in Akasaka, 1984; Commercial Environment Design Award for Pavilion, 1985; Commercial Environment Design Award for the Act Six, 1986; Kitakyushu City Architectural Culture Award for the NRCC, 1987; Architectural Institute of Japan Award, 1989; Iaks Award, Gold Medal, 1993; Finalist, Benedictus Award, 1994. Yoh has also been a Lecturer at the Architecture Department of Kyushu University since 1992 and was a Visiting Professor of Architecture at the Graduate School of Architecture, Planning and Preservation at Columbia University, New York, in 1992. He is also Professor of Architecture and Urban Design at the Graduate School of Keio Gijnkn University since 1996.